5/20/96 Baker + Taylor 26.96

Modern Critical Views

Chinua Achebe
Henry Adams
Aeschylus
S. Y. Agnon
Edward Albee
Raphael Alberti
Louisa May Alcott
A. R. Ammons
Sherwood Anderson
Aristophanes
Matthew Arnold
Antonin Artaud
John Ashbery
Margaret Atwood
W. H. Auden
Jane Austen
Isaac Babel
Sir Francis Bacon
James Baldwin
Honoré de Balzac
John Barth
Donald Barthelme
Charles Baudelaire
Simone de Beauvoir
Samuel Beckett
Saul Bellow
Thomas Berger
John Berryman
The Bible
Elizabeth Bishop
William Blake
Giovanni Boccaccio
Heinrich Böll
Jorge Luis Borges
Elizabeth Bowen
Bertolt Brecht
The Brontës
Charles Brockden Brown
Sterling Brown
Robert Browning
Martin Buber
John Bunyan
Anthony Burgess
Kenneth Burke
Robert Burns
William Burroughs
George Gordon, Lord
  Byron
Pedro Calderón de la Barca
Italo Calvino
Albert Camus
Canadian Poetry: Modern
  and Contemporary
Canadian Poetry through
  E. J. Pratt
Thomas Carlyle
Alejo Carpentier
Lewis Carroll
Willa Cather
Louis-Ferdinand Céline
Miguel de Cervantes

Geoffrey Chaucer
John Cheever
Anton Chekhov
Kate Chopin
Chrétien de Troyes
Agatha Christie
Samuel Taylor Coleridge
Colette
William Congreve & the
  Restoration Dramatists
Joseph Conrad
Contemporary Poets
James Fenimore Cooper
Pierre Corneille
Julio Cortázar
Hart Crane
Stephen Crane
e. e. cummings
Dante
Robertson Davies
Daniel Defoe
Philip K. Dick
Charles Dickens
James Dickey
Emily Dickinson
Denis Diderot
Isak Dinesen
E. L. Doctorow
John Donne & the
  Seventeenth-Century
  Metaphysical Poets
John Dos Passos
Fyodor Dostoevsky
Frederick Douglass
Theodore Dreiser
John Dryden
W. E. B. Du Bois
Lawrence Durrell
George Eliot
T. S. Eliot
Elizabethan Dramatists
Ralph Ellison
Ralph Waldo Emerson
Euripides
William Faulkner
Henry Fielding
F. Scott Fitzgerald
Gustave Flaubert
E. M. Forster
John Fowles
Sigmund Freud
Robert Frost
Northrop Frye
Carlos Fuentes
William Gaddis
Federico García Lorca
Gabriel García Márquez
André Gide
W. S. Gilbert
Allen Ginsberg
J. W. von Goethe

Nikolai Gogol
William Golding
Oliver Goldsmith
Mary Gordon
Günther Grass
Robert Graves
Graham Greene
Thomas Hardy
Nathaniel Hawthorne
William Hazlitt
H. D.
Seamus Heaney
Lillian Hellman
Ernest Hemingway
Hermann Hesse
Geoffrey Hill
Friedrich Hölderlin
Homer
A. D. Hope
Gerard Manley Hopkins
Horace
A. E. Housman
William Dean Howells
Langston Hughes
Ted Hughes
Victor Hugo
Zora Neale Hurston
Aldous Huxley
Henrik Ibsen
Eugène Ionesco
Washington Irving
Henry James
Dr. Samuel Johnson and
  James Boswell
Ben Jonson
James Joyce
Carl Gustav Jung
Franz Kafka
Yasonari Kawabata
John Keats
Søren Kierkegaard
Rudyard Kipling
Melanie Klein
Heinrich von Kleist
Philip Larkin
D. H. Lawrence
John le Carré
Ursula K. Le Guin
Giacomo Leopardi
Doris Lessing
Sinclair Lewis
Jack London
Robert Lowell
Malcolm Lowry
Carson McCullers
Norman Mailer
Bernard Malamud
Stéphane Mallarmé
Sir Thomas Malory
André Malraux
Thomas Mann

Modern Critical Views

Katherine Mansfield
Christopher Marlowe
Andrew Marvell
Herman Melville
George Meredith
James Merrill
John Stuart Mill
Arthur Miller
Henry Miller
John Milton
Yukio Mishima
Molière
Michel de Montaigne
Eugenio Montale
Marianne Moore
Alberto Moravia
Toni Morrison
Alice Munro
Iris Murdoch
Robert Musil
Vladimir Nabokov
V. S. Naipaul
R. K. Narayan
Pablo Neruda
John Henry Newman
Friedrich Nietzsche
Frank Norris
Joyce Carol Oates
Sean O'Casey
Flannery O'Connor
Christopher Okigbo
Charles Olson
Eugene O'Neill
José Ortega y Gasset
Joe Orton
George Orwell
Ovid
Wilfred Owen
Amos Oz
Cynthia Ozick
Grace Paley
Blaise Pascal
Walter Pater
Octavio Paz
Walker Percy
Petrarch
Pindar
Harold Pinter
Luigi Pirandello
Sylvia Plath
Plato

Plautus
Edgar Allan Poe
Poets of Sensibility & the
  Sublime
Poets of the Nineties
Alexander Pope
Katherine Anne Porter
Ezra Pound
Anthony Powell
Pre-Raphaelite Poets
Marcel Proust
Manuel Puig
Alexander Pushkin
Thomas Pynchon
Francisco de Quevedo
François Rabelais
Jean Racine
Ishmael Reed
Adrienne Rich
Samuel Richardson
Mordecai Richler
Rainer Maria Rilke
Arthur Rimbaud
Edwin Arlington Robinson
Theodore Roethke
Philip Roth
Jean-Jacques Rousseau
John Ruskin
J. D. Salinger
Jean-Paul Sartre
Gershom Scholem
Sir Walter Scott
William Shakespeare
  Histories & Poems
  Comedies & Romances
  Tragedies
George Bernard Shaw
Mary Wollstonecraft
  Shelley
Percy Bysshe Shelley
Sam Shepard
Richard Brinsley Sheridan
Sir Philip Sidney
Isaac Bashevis Singer
Tobias Smollett
Alexander Solzhenitsyn
Sophocles
Wole Soyinka
Edmund Spenser
Gertrude Stein
John Steinbeck

Stendhal
Laurence Sterne
Wallace Stevens
Robert Louis Stevenson
Tom Stoppard
August Strindberg
Jonathan Swift
John Millington Synge
Alfred, Lord Tennyson
William Makepeace Thackeray
Dylan Thomas
Henry David Thoreau
James Thurber and S. J.
  Perelman
J. R. R. Tolkien
Leo Tolstoy
Jean Toomer
Lionel Trilling
Anthony Trollope
Ivan Turgenev
Mark Twain
Miguel de Unamuno
John Updike
Paul Valéry
Cesar Vallejo
Lope de Vega
Gore Vidal
Virgil
Voltaire
Kurt Vonnegut
Derek Walcott
Alice Walker
Robert Penn Warren
Evelyn Waugh
H. G. Wells
Eudora Welty
Nathanael West
Edith Wharton
Patrick White
Walt Whitman
Oscar Wilde
Tennessee Williams
William Carlos Williams
Thomas Wolfe
Virginia Woolf
William Wordsworth
Jay Wright
Richard Wright
William Butler Yeats
A. B. Yehoshua
Emile Zola

Modern Critical Views

KATE CHOPIN

Edited and with an introduction by
Harold Bloom
Sterling Professor of the Humanities
Yale University

CHELSEA HOUSE PUBLISHERS
New York ◇ Philadelphia

Library of Congress Cataloging-in-Publication Data
Kate Chopin.
    (Modern critical views)
    Bibliography: p.
    Includes index.
    Contents: A forgotten novel / Kenneth Eble—An
abyss of inequality / Larzer Ziff—Cane River world /
Donald A. Ringe — [etc.]
    1. Chopin, Kate, 1851–1904—Criticism and
interpretation. [1. Chopin, Kate, 1851–1904—Criticism
and interpretation. 2. American literature—History and
criticism]. I. Bloom, Harold. II. Series.
PS1294.C63K38 1986   813'.4   86–20688
ISBN 0–87754–693–2

Contents

Editor's Note

This volume brings together what I judge to be the best criticism devoted to the fiction of Kate Chopin, reprinted here in the chronological order of its original publication. I am grateful to Peter Childers for his assistance in editing this volume.

My introduction concerns itself with the relation of *The Awakening* to the poetry of Walt Whitman, which I believe provided Chopin with the autoerotic vision (as I take it to be) of her novel. Kenneth Eble begins the chronological sequence with his early revaluation of *The Awakening* as an unjustly "forgotten novel." In a contextualization of the book that relates it to the literary scene of the American 1890s, Larzer Ziff insists upon Chopin's Flaubertian "detachment" in regard to Edna Pontellier's fate.

Donald A. Ringe, addressing himself to Chopin's first novel, *At Fault*, and her earliest Creole short stories, attempts to make an aesthetic case for them. Her best known story, "Désirée's Baby," is interpreted by Cynthia Griffin Wolff as a vision that confronts "the bleak fact of life's tenuous stabilities." We return to *The Awakening* with the essay by Susan J. Rosowski, who reads the novel from a feminist perspective, so that Edna becomes the victim of a society that allows her only the roles and values it assigns to women, not to fully human beings.

Joyce Dyer follows with two pieces on Chopin, the first on a recurrent figure (Gouvernail, the sensitive bachelor) in her work, and the second on younger males, whom she portrays as undergoing "awakenings" similar to Edna's. In a consideration of the sketch "Ripe Figs," Elaine Gardiner uncovers Chopin in miniature, through a circular parable of sensual maturation.

Our most eminent feminist critic, Sandra M. Gilbert, contributes a comprehensive and profound exegesis of the mythic pattern of *The Awakening*.

A subtle consideration of Adèle's role as siren in *The Awakening,* by Kathleen Margaret Lant, concludes this volume with another tragic reading of the novel, one in which "Edna awakens to the horrible knowledge that she can never, because she is female, be her own person."

Introduction

The Complete Works of Kate Chopin (1969) comprise only two volumes. In her own lifetime (1851–1904), she published two novels, *At Fault* (1890), which I have not read, and the now celebrated *The Awakening* (1899), as well as two volumes of short stories, *Bayou Folk* (1894) and *A Night in Acadie* (1897). The short stories—out of Maupassant—are very mixed in quality, but even the best are fairly slight. *The Awakening,* a flawed but strong novel, now enjoys an eminent status among feminist critics, but I believe that many of them weakly misread the book, which is anything but feminist in its stance. It is a Whitmanian book, profoundly so, not only in its echoes of his poetry, which are manifold, but more crucially in its erotic perspective, which is narcissistic and even autoerotic, very much in Whitman's true mode. The sexual awakening that centers the novel involves a narcissistic self-investment that constitutes a new ego for the heroine. Unfortunately, she fails to see that her passion is for herself, and this error perhaps destroys her.

Lest I seem ironic, here at the start, I protest that irony is hardly my trope; that Walt Whitman, in my judgment, remains the greatest American writer; and that I continue to admire *The Awakening,* though a bit less at the second reading than at the first. Its faults are mostly in its diction; Chopin had no mastery of style. As narrative, it is simplistic rather than simple, and its characters have nothing memorable about them. Chopin's exuberance as a writer was expended where we would expect a daughter of Whitman to locate her concern: the ecstatic rebirth of the self. Since Chopin was not writing either American epic or American elegy, but rather an everyday domestic novel, more naturalistic than Romantic, fissures were bound to appear in her work. The form of Flaubert does not accommodate what Emerson—who may be called Chopin's literary grandfather—named as the great and

1

crescive self. Nevertheless, as a belated American Transcendentalist, Chopin
risked the experiment, and what Emerson called the Newness breaks the
vessels of Chopin's chosen form. I would call this the novel's largest strength,
though it is also its formal weakness.

II

Walt Whitman the man doubtless lusted after what he termed the love
of comrades, but Walt Whitman the poet persuades us rhetorically only when
he lusts after himself. To state this more precisely, Walt Whitman, one of
the roughs, an American, the self of *Song of Myself,* lusts after "the real me"
or "me myself" of Walt Whitman. Chopin's heroine, Edna, becomes, as it
were, one of the roughs, an American, when she allows herself to lust after
her real me, her me myself. That is why Chopin's *The Awakening* gave offense
to reviewers in 1899, precisely as *Leaves of Grass* gave offense from its first
appearance in 1855, onwards to Whitman's death, and would still give offense, if we read it as the Pindaric celebration of masturbation that it truly
constitutes. Edna, like Walt, falls in love with her own body, and her infatuation with the inadequate Robert is merely a screen for her overwhelming
obsession, which is to nurse and mother herself. Chopin, on some level, must
have known how sublimely outrageous she was being, but the level was not
overt, and part of her novel's power is in its negation of its own deepest
knowledge. Her reviewers were not stupid, and it is shallow to condemn
them, as some feminist critics now tend to do. Here is the crucial paragraph
in a review by one Frances Porcher (in *The Mirror* 9, May 4, 1899), who
senses obscurely but accurately that Edna's desire is for herself:

> It is not a pleasant picture of soul-dissection, take it anyway you
> like; and so, though she finally kills herself, or rather lets herself
> drown to death, one feels that it is not in the desperation born
> of an over-burdened heart, torn by complicating duties but rather
> because she realizes that something is due to her children, that
> she cannot get away from, and she is too weak to face the issue.
> Besides which, and this is the stronger feeling, she has offered
> herself wholly to the man, who loves her too well to take her at
> her word; "she realizes that the day would come when he, too,
> and the thought of him, would melt out of her existence," she
> has awakened to know the shifting, treacherous, fickle deeps of
> her own soul in which lies, alert and strong and cruel, the fiend
> called Passion that is all animal and all of the earth, earthy. It is

better to lie down in the green waves and sink down in close embraces of old ocean, and so she does.

The metaphor of "shifting, treacherous, fickle deeps" here, however unoriginal, clearly pertains more to Edna's body than to her soul, and what is most "alert and strong and cruel" in Edna is manifestly a passion for herself. The love-death that Edna dies has its Wagnerian element, but again is more Whitmanian, suggesting the song of death sung by the hermit thrush or solitary singer in "When Lilacs Last in the Dooryard Bloom'd." Edna moves in the heavy, sensual and sensuous atmosphere of Whitman's "The Sleepers," and she dies only perhaps as Whitman's real me or me myself dies, awash in a body indistinguishable from her own, the body of the mother, death, the ocean, and the night of a narcissistic dream of love that perfectly restitutes the self for all its losses, that heals fully the original, narcissistic scar.

Sandra M. Gilbert, who seems to me our most accomplished feminist critic, reads the novel as a female revision of the male aesthetic reveries of Aphrodite's rebirth. I would revise Gilbert only by suggesting that the major instances of such reverie—in Dante Gabriel Rossetti, Swinburne, Pater, and Wilde—are not less female than Chopin's vision is, and paradoxically are more feminist than her version of the myth. The autoerotic seems to be a realm where, metaphorically anyway, there are no major differences between male and female seers, so that Chopin's representation of Edna's psychic self-gratification is not essentially altered from Whitman's solitary bliss:

> Edna, left alone in the little side room, loosened her clothes, re-
> moving the greater part of them. She bathed her face, her neck
> and arms in the basin that stood between the windows. She took
> off her shoes and stockings and stretched herself in the very center
> of the high, white bed. How luxurious it felt to rest thus in a
> strange, quaint bed, with its sweet country odor of laurel linger-
> ing about the sheets and mattress! She stretched her strong limbs
> that ached a little. She ran her fingers through her loosened hair
> for a while. She looked at her round arms as she held them
> straight up and rubbed them one after the other, observing
> closely, as if it were something she saw for the first time, the fine,
> firm quality and texture of her flesh. She clasped her hands easily
> above her head, and it was thus she fell asleep.

Edna observing, as a discovery, "the fine, firm quality and texture of her flesh," is the heir of Whitman proclaiming: "If I worship one thing more

than another it shall be the spread of my own body, or any part of it."
Chopin seems to have understood, better than most readers in 1899, what
Whitman meant by his crucial image of the tally: "My knowledge my live
parts, it keeping tally with the meaning of all things." As the erotic image
of the poet's voice, the tally obeys Emerson's dark law of Compensation:
"Nothing is got for nothing." If Edna awakens to her own passion for her
own body and its erotic potential, then she must come also to the tally's
measurement of her own death.

III

Some aspects of Whitman's influence upon *The Awakening* have been
traced by Lewis Leary and others, but since the influence is not always overt
but frequently repressed, there is more to be noticed about it. Edna first
responds to "the everlasting voice of the sea" in chapter 4, where its maternal
contrast to her husband's not unkind inadequacy causes her to weep copi-
ously. At the close of chapter 6, the voice of the Whitmanian ocean is directly
associated with Edna's awakening to self:

> The voice of the sea is seductive; never ceasing, whispering, clam-
> oring, murmuring, inviting the soul to wander for a spell in
> abysses of solitude; to lose itself in mazes of inward contempla-
> tion.
>   The voice of the sea speaks to the soul. The touch of the sea
> is sensuous, enfolding the body in its soft, close embrace.

This is a palpable and overt influence; far subtler, because repressed, is
the Whitmanian aura with which Kate Chopin associates the ambivalence
of motherhood. Whitman himself both fathered and mothered all of his
mostly tormented siblings, as soon as he was able, but his own ambivalences
toward both fatherhood and motherhood inform much of his best poetry.
Something of the ambiguous strength of *The Awakening*'s conclusion hovers
in its repressed relation to Whitman. Edna leaves Robert, after their mutual
declaration of love, in order to attend her close friend Adèle in her labor
pains:

> Edna began to feel uneasy. She was seized with a vague dread.
> Her own like experiences seemed far away, unreal, and only half
> remembered. She recalled faintly an ecstasy of pain, the heavy
> odor of chloroform, a stupor which had deadened sensation, and
> an awakening to find a little new life to which she had given

being, added to the great unnumbered multitude of souls that come and go.

　　She began to wish she had not come; her presence was not necessary. She might have invented a pretext for staying away; she might even invent a pretext now for going. But Edna did not go. With an inward agony, with a flaming, outspoken revolt against the ways of Nature, she witnessed the scene [of] torture.

　　She was still stunned and speechless with emotion when later she leaned over her friend to kiss her and softly say good-by. Adèle, pressing her cheek, whispered in an exhausted voice: "Think of the children, Edna. Oh think of the children! Remember them!"

The protest against nature here is hardly equivocal, yet it has the peculiar numbness of "the great unnumbered multitude of souls that come and go." Schopenhauer's influence joins Whitman's as Chopin shows us Edna awakening to the realization of lost individuality, of not wanting "anything but my own way," while knowing that the will to live insists always upon its own way, at the individual's expense:

Despondency had come upon her there in the wakeful night, and had never lifted. There was no one thing in the world that she desired. There was no human being whom she wanted near her except Robert; and she even realized that the day would come when he, too, and the thought of him would melt out of her existence, leaving her alone. The children appeared before her like antagonists who had overcome her; who had overpowered and sought to drag her into the soul's slavery for the rest of her days. But she knew a way to elude them. She was not thinking of these things when she walked down to the beach.

　　The water of the Gulf stretched out before her, gleaming with the million lights of the sun. The voice of the sea is seductive, never ceasing, whispering, clamoring, murmuring, inviting the soul to wander in abysses of solitude. All along the white beach, up and down, there was no living thing in sight. A bird with a broken wing was beating the air above, reeling, fluttering, circling disabled down, down to the water.

The soul's slavery, in Schopenhauer, is to be eluded through philosophical contemplation of a very particular kind, but in Whitman only through a dangerous liaison with night, death, the mother, and the sea. Chopin is closer again to Whitman, and the image of the disabled bird circling down-ward to darkness stations itself between Whitman and Wallace Stevens, as it were, and constitutes another American approach to the Emersonian abyss of the self. Edna, stripped naked, enters the mothering sea with another recall of Whitman: "The foamy wavelets curled up to her white feet, and coiled like serpents about her ankles." In the hermit thrush's great song of death that is the apotheosis of "When Lilacs Last in the Dooryard Bloom'd," death arrives coiled and curled like a serpent, undulating round the world. Whitman's "dark mother always gliding near with soft feet" has come to deliver Edna from the burden of being a mother, and indeed from all burden of otherness, forever.

KENNETH EBLE

A Forgotten Novel

When Kate Chopin's novel *The Awakening* was published in 1899, it made its mark on American letters principally in the reactions it provoked among shocked newspaper reviewers. In St. Louis, Mrs. Chopin's native city, the book was taken from circulation at the Mercantile Library, and though by this time she had established herself as one of the city's most talented writers, she was now denied membership in the Fine Arts Club. The St. Louis *Republic* said the novel was, like most of Mrs. Chopin's work, "too strong drink for moral babes and should be labeled 'poison.'" The *Nation* granted its "fine workmanship and pellucid style," but went on, "We cannot see that literature or the criticism of life is helped by the detailed history of the manifold and contemporary love affairs of a wife and mother."

After Mrs. Chopin's death in 1904, a story passed from the *Library of Southern Literature* through F. L. Pattee's *American Literature since 1870* and into the *Dictionary of American Biography* that Kate Chopin's brief writing career came to an abrupt end in her bitter disappointment over the reception of *The Awakening*. The story is false—her manuscript collection shows that she wrote six stories after 1900, three of which were published. But the implications are probably accurate. There is little doubt of the squeamishness of American literary taste in 1900, nor is there much doubt that Kate Chopin was deeply hurt by the attacks on the novel as well as on her own motives and morals. The stories she wrote thereafter lack distinction,

From *Western Humanities Review* 10, no. 3 (Summer 1956). © 1956 by the University of Utah.

and though *The Awakening* was reprinted by Duffield and Company in 1906, it is likely that the author's innocent disregard for contemporary moral delicacies ordained that it should be quickly forgotten.

Today, Kate (O'Flaherty) Chopin is chiefly remembered as a regional writer whose short stories of the Louisiana Creoles are usually compared with the work of George Washington Cable and Grace King. Her writing career is unusual for its brevity: it began in 1889 and ended with her death in 1904. She did not publish until she was thirty-nine, although it is apparent that in the preceding years she read widely and took some pride in her writing as well as in her discriminating tastes in music, art and literature. Given other circumstances, she might have developed into a writer early in her life. As it was, the talent she possessed was quite simply submerged as the result of an early and happy marriage and the raising of a sizable family.

She was born in St. Louis in 1851, educated in a convent school, moved to New Orleans when she married Oscar Chopin in 1870, and there became the mother of six children in the next ten years. She returned to St. Louis after her husband died in 1882, but her life in New Orleans and in Natchitoches Parish, where she lived for two years immediately before her husband's death, gave her most of her fictional material. Her husband's estate was small, and the O'Flaherty family estate had dwindled by the time of her mother's death in 1885. Left alone with a family to support, she may have turned seriously to writing because of a feeling of necessity. From 1889 until her death, her stories and miscellaneous writings appeared in *Vogue, Youth's Companion, Atlantic Monthly, Century, Saturday Evening Post,* and many lesser publications. Her books, in addition to *The Awakening,* are *At Fault* (1890), a novel, and two collections of stories and sketches, *Bayou Folk* (1894) and *A Night in Acadie* (1897).

Her present literary rank is probably somewhere between Octave Thanet (Alice French) and Sarah Orne Jewett. In the fifty years after her death, she has provoked two articles and a doctoral dissertation on her life and work. Her own books are long out of print, and *The Awakening* is particularly hard to find. Their disappearance is not unusual; it is inevitable that much of a minor writer's work will be lost. What is unfortunate is that *The Awakening,* certainly Mrs. Chopin's best work, has been neglected almost from its publication.

The claim of the book upon the reader's attention is simple. It is a first-rate novel. The justification for urging its importance is that we have few enough novels of its stature. One could add that it is advanced in theme and technique over the novels of its day, and that it anticipates in many respects the modern novel. It could be claimed that it adds to American fiction an example of what Gide called the *roman pur,* a kind of novel not characteristic of American writing. One could offer the book as evidence that the regional writer can go beyond the limitations of regional material. But these matters aside, what recommends the novel is its general excellence.

It is surprising that the book has not been picked up today by reprint houses long on lurid covers and short on new talent. The nature of its theme, which had much to do with its adverse reception in 1899, would offer little offense today. In a way, the novel is an American *Bovary,* though such a designation is not precisely accurate. Its central character is similar: the married woman who seeks love outside a stuffy, middle-class marriage. It is similar too in the definitive way it portrays the mind of a woman trapped in marriage and seeking fulfillment of what she vaguely recognizes as her essential nature. The husband, Léonce Pontellier, is a businessman whose nature and preoccupations are not far different from those of Charles Bovary. There is a Léon Dupuis in Robert Lebrun, a Rodolphe Boulanger in Alcée Arobin. And too, like *Madame Bovary,* the novel handles its material superbly well. Kate Chopin herself was probably more than any other American writer of her time under French influence. Her background was French-Irish; she married a Creole; she read and spoke French and knew contemporary French literature well; she associated both in St. Louis and Louisiana with families of French ancestry and disposition. But despite the similarities and possible influences, the novel, chiefly because of the independent character of its heroine, Edna Pontellier, and because of the intensity of the focus upon her, is not simply a good but derivative work. It has a manner and matter of its own.

Quite frankly, the book is about sex. Not only is it about sex, but the very texture of the writing is sensuous, if not sensual, from the first to the last. Even as late as 1932, Chopin's biographer, Daniel Rankin, seemed somewhat shocked by it. He paid his respects to the artistic excellence of the book, but he was troubled by "that insistent query—*cui bono?*" He called the novel "exotic in setting, morbid in theme, erotic in motivation." One questions the accuracy of these terms, and even more the moral disapproval implied in their usage. One regrets that Mr. Rankin did not emphasize that the book was amazingly honest, perceptive and moving.

The Awakening is a study of Edna Pontellier, a story, as the *Nation* criticized it, "of a Southern lady who wanted to do what she wanted to. From wanting to, she did, with disastrous consequences." Such a succinct statement, blunt but accurate so far as it goes, may suggest that a detailed retelling of the story would convey little of the actual character of the novel. It is, of course, one of those novels a person simply must read to gain any real impression of its excellence. But the compactness of the work in narrative, characterization, setting, symbols and images gives meaning to such an imprecise and overworked expression. Some idea of the style may be conveyed by quoting the opening paragraphs:

> A green and yellow parrot, which hung in a cage outside the door, kept repeating over and over "*Allez vous-en! Allez vous-en! Sapristi!* That's all right."
>
> He could speak a little Spanish, and also a language which nobody understood, unless it was the mockingbird that hung on the other side of the door, whistling his fluty notes out upon the breeze with maddening persistence.
>
> Mr. Pontellier, unable to read his newspaper with any degree of comfort, arose with an expression and an exclamation of disgust. He walked down the gallery and across the narrow "bridges" which connected the Lebrun cottages one with the other. He had been seated before the door of the main house. The parrot and the mockingbird were the property of Madame Lebrun and they had the right to make all the noise they wished. Mr. Pontellier had the privilege of quitting their society when they ceased to be entertaining.

This is Mr. Pontellier. He is a businessman, husband and father, not given to romance, not given to much of anything outside his business. When he comes to Grand Isle, the summer place of the Creoles in the story, he is anxious to get back to his cotton brokerage in Carondelet Street, New Orleans, and he passes his time on Grand Isle at the hotel smoking his cigars and playing cards. When he is on the beach at all, he is not a participant, but a watcher.

> He fixed his gaze upon a white sunshade that was advancing at snail's pace from the beach. He could see it plainly between the gaunt trunk of the water-oaks and across the strip of yellow camomile. The gulf looked far away, melting hazily into the blue of the horizon. The sunshade continued to approach slowly. Beneath its pink-lined shelter were their faces, Mrs. Pontellier and young Robert Lebrun.

It is apparent that a triangle has been formed, and going into the details of the subsequent events in a summary fashion would likely destroy the art by which such a sequence becomes significant. Suffice to say that Robert Lebrun is the young man who first awakens, or rather, is present at the awakening of Edna Pontellier into passion, a passion which Mr. Pontellier neither understands nor appreciates. Slowly Edna and Robert fall in love, but once again, the expression is too trite. Edna grows into an awareness of a woman's physical nature, and Robert is actually but a party of the second part. The reader's attention is never allowed to stray from Edna. At the climax of their relationship, young Lebrun recognizes what must follow and goes away. During his absence, Mrs. Pontellier becomes idly amused by a roué, Arobin, and, becoming more than amused, more than tolerates his advances. When Robert returns he finds that Edna is willing to declare her love and accept the consequences of her passion. But Robert, abiding by the traditional romantic code which separates true love from physical passion, refuses the offered consummation. When he leaves Mrs. Pontellier, she turns once again to the scene of her awakening, the sand and sea of Grand Isle:

> The water of the Gulf stretched out before her, gleaming with the million lights of the sun. The voice of the sea is seductive, never ceasing, whispering, clamoring, murmuring, inviting the soul to wander in abysses of solitude. All along the white beach, up and down, there was no living thing in sight. A bird with a broken wing was beating the air above, reeling, fluttering, circling disabled down, down to the water.
>
> Edna had found her old bathing suit still hanging, faded, upon its accustomed peg.
>
> She put it on, left her clothing in the bath-house. But when she was there beside the sea, absolutely alone, she cast the unpleasant, pricking garments from her, and for the first time in her life she stood naked in the open air at the mercy of the sun, the breeze that beat upon her, and the waves that invited her.
>
> How strange and awful it seemed to stand naked under the sky! How delicious! She felt like some newborn creature, opening its eye in a familiar world that it had never known.
>
> The foamy wavelets curled up to her white feet, and coiled like serpents about her ankles. She walked out. The water was chill, but she walked on. The water was deep, but she lifted her white body and reached out with a long, sweeping stroke. The touch of the sea is sensuous, enfolding the body in its soft close embrace. . . .
>
> She looked into the distance, and the old terror flamed up for an instant, then sank again. Edna heard her father's voice and her sister Margaret's. She heard the barking of an old dog that

was chained to the sycamore tree. The spurs of the cavalry officer clanged as he walked across the porch. There was the hum of bees, and the musty odor of pinks filled the air.

Here is the story, its beginning a mature woman's awakening to physical love, its end her walking into the sea. The extracts convey something of the author's style, but much less of the movement of the characters and of human desire against the sensuous background of sea and sand. Looking at the novel analytically, one can say that it excels chiefly in its characterizations and its structure, the use of images and symbols to unify that structure, and the character of Edna Pontellier.

Kate Chopin, almost from her first story, had the ability to capture character, to put the right word in the mouth, to impart the exact gesture, to select the characteristic action. An illustration of her deftness in handling even minor characters is her treatment of Edna's father. When he leaves the Pontellier's after a short visit, Edna is glad to be rid of him and "his padded shoulders, his Bible reading, his 'toddies,' and ponderous oaths." A moment later, it is a side of Edna's nature which is revealed. She felt a sense of relief at her father's absence; "she read Emerson until she grew sleepy."

Characterization was always Mrs. Chopin's talent. Structure was not. Those who knew her working habits say that she seldom revised, and she herself mentions that she did not like reworking her stories. Though her reputation rests upon her short narratives, her collected stories give abundant evidence of the sketch, the outlines of stories which remain unformed. And when she did attempt a tightly organized story, she often turned to Maupassant and was as likely as not to effect a contrived symmetry. Her early novel *At Fault* suffers most from her inability to control her material. In *The Awakening* she is in complete command of structure. She seems to have grasped instinctively the use of the unifying symbol—here the sea, sky and sand—and with it the power of individual images to bind the story together.

The sea, the sand, the sun and sky of the Gulf Coast become almost a presence themselves in the novel. Much of the sensuousness of the book comes from the way the reader is never allowed to stray far from the water's edge. A refrain beginning "The voice of the sea is seductive, never ceasing, clamoring, murmuring" is used throughout the novel. It appears first at the beginning of Edna Pontellier's awakening, and it appears at the end as the introduction to the long final scene, previously quoted. Looking closely at the final form of this refrain, one can notice the care with which Mrs. Chopin composed this theme and variation. In the initial statement, the sentence does not end with "solitude," but goes on, as it should, "to lose itself in mazes of inward contemplation." Nor is the image of the bird with the broken wing in the earlier passage; rather there is a prefiguring of the final tragedy: "The voice of the sea speaks to the soul. The touch of the sea is sensuous, enfolding the body in its soft close embrace." The way scene, mood, action and character are fused reminds one not so much of literature as of an impressionist painting, of a Renoir with much of the sweetness missing. Only Stephen Crane, among her American contemporaries, had an equal sensitivity to light and shadow, color and texture, had the painter's eye matched with the writer's perception of character and incident.

The best example of Mrs. Chopin's use of a visual image which is also highly symbolic is the lady in black and the two nameless lovers. They are seen as touches of paint upon the canvas and as indistinct yet evocative figures which accompany Mrs. Pontellier and Robert Lebrun during the course of their intimacy. They appear first early in the novel. "The lady in black was reading her morning devotions on the porch of a neighboring bath house. Two young lovers were exchanging their heart's yearning beneath the children's tent which they had found unoccupied." Throughout the course of Edna's awakening, these figures appear and reappear, the lovers entering the pension, leaning toward each other as the water-oaks bent from the sea, the lady in black, creeping behind them. They accompany Edna and Robert when they first go to the Chênière, "the lovers, shoulder to shoulder, creeping, the lady in black, gaining steadily upon them." When Robert departs for Mexico, the picture changes. Lady and lovers depart together, and Edna finds herself back from the sea and shore, and set among her human acquaintances, her husband; her father; Mme. Reisz, the musician, "a homely woman with a small wizened face and body, and eyes that glowed"; Alcée Arobin; Mme. Ragtinolle; and others. One brief scene from this milieu will further illustrate Mrs. Chopin's conscious or unconscious symbolism.

The climax of Edna's relationship with Arobin is the dinner which is to celebrate her last night in her and her husband's house. Edna is ready to move to a small place around the corner where she can escape (though she does not phrase it this way) the feeling that she is one more of Léonce Pontellier's possessions. At the dinner Victor Lebrun, Robert's brother, begins singing, "Ah! si tu savais!" a song which brings back all her memories of Robert. She sets her glass so blindly down that she shatters it against the carafe. "The wine spilled over Arobin's legs and some of it trickled down upon Mrs. Highcamp's black gauze gown." After the other guests have gone, Edna and Arobin walk to the new house. Mrs. Chopin writes of Edna, "She looked down, noticing the black line of his leg moving in and out so close to her against the yellow shimmer of her gown." The chapter concludes:

His hand had strayed to her beautiful shoulders, and he could feel the response of her flesh to his touch. He seated himself beside her and kissed her lightly upon the shoulder.

"I thought you were going away," she said, in an uneven voice.

"I am, after I have said good night."

"Good night," she murmured.

He did not answer, except to continue to caress her. He did not say good night until she had become supple to his gentle, seductive entreaties.

It is not surprising that the sensuous quality of the book, both from the incidents of the novel and the symbolic implications, would have offended contemporary reviewers. What convinced many critics of the indecency of the book, however, was not simply the sensuous scenes, but rather that the author obviously sympathized with Mrs. Pontellier. More than that, the readers probably found that she aroused their own sympathies.

It is a letter from an English reader which states most clearly, in a matter-of-fact way, the importance of Edna Pontellier. The letter was to Kate Chopin from Lady Janet Scammon Young, and included a more interesting analysis of the novel by Dr. Dunrobin Thomson, a London physician whom Lady Janet said a great editor had called "the soundest critic since Matthew Arnold." "That which makes *The Awakening* legitimate," Dr. Thomson wrote, "is that the author deals with the commonest of human experiences. You fancy *Edna's* case exceptional? Trust an old doctor—most common." He goes on to speak of the "abominable prudishness" masquerading as "modesty or virtue," which makes the woman who marries a victim. For passion is regarded as disgraceful and the self-respecting female assumes she does not possess passion. "In so far as normally constituted womanhood *must* take account of something *sexual*," he points out, "it is called love." But marital love and passion may not be one. The wise husband, Dr. Thomson advises, seeing within his wife the "mysterious affinity" between a married woman and a man who stirs her passions, will help her see the distinction between her heart and her love, which wifely loyalty owes to the husband, and her body, which yearns for awakening. But more than clinically analyzing the discrepancy between Victorian morals and woman's nature, Dr. Thomson testifies that Mrs. Chopin has not been false or sensational to no purpose. He does not feel that she has corrupted, nor does he regard the warring within Edna's self as insignificant.

Greek tragedy—to remove ourselves from Victorian morals—knew well *eros* was not the kind of *love* which can be easily prettified and sentimentalized. Phaedra's struggle with elemental passion in the *Hippolytus* is not generally regarded as being either morally offensive or insignificant. Mrs. Pontellier, too, has the power, the dignity, the self-possession of a tragic heroine. She is not an Emma Bovary, deluded by ideas of "romance," nor is she the sensuous but guilt-ridden woman of the sensational novel. We can find only partial reason for her affair in the kind of romantic desire to escape a middle-class existence which animates Emma Bovary. Edna Pontellier is neither deluded nor deludes. She is woman, the physical woman who, despite her Kentucky Presbyterian upbringing and a comfortable marriage, must struggle with the sensual appeal of physical ripeness itself, with passion of which she is only dimly aware. Her struggle is not melodramatic, nor is it artificial, nor vapid. It is objective, real and moving. And when she walks into the sea, it does not leave a reader with the sense of sin punished, but rather with the sense evoked by Edwin Arlington Robinson's *Eros Turannos:*

> for they
> That with a god have striven
> Not hearing much of what we say,
> Take what the god has given;
> Though like waves breaking it may be,
> Or like a changed familiar tree,
> Or like a stairway to the sea
> Where down the blind are driven.

How wrong to call Edna, as Daniel Rankin does, "a selfish, capricious" woman. Rather, Edna's struggle, the struggle with *eros* itself, is farthest removed from capriciousness. It is her self-awareness, and her awakening into a greater degree of self-awareness than those around her can comprehend, which gives her story dignity and significance.

Our advocacy of the novel is not meant to obscure its faults. It is not perfect art, but in total effect it provokes few dissatisfactions. A sophisticated modern reader might find something of the derivative about it. Kate Chopin read widely, and a list of novelists she found interesting would include Flaubert, Tolstoy, Turgenev, D'Annunzio, Bourget, Goncourt and Zola. It is doubtful, however, that there was any direct borrowing, and *The Awakening* exists, as do most good novels, as a product of the author's literary, real, and imagined life.

How Mrs. Chopin managed to create in ten years the substantial body of work she achieved is no less a mystery than the excellence of *The Awak-*

ening itself. But, having added to American literature a novel uncommon in its kind as in its excellence, she deserves not to be forgotten. *The Awakening* deserves to be restored and to be given its place among novels worthy of preservation.

An Abyss of Inequality

Kate Chopin was born Katharine O'Flaherty in Saint Louis in 1851 and was raised in a family sympathetic to the Confederacy. Her mother was French, and she learned the language at home and at her convent school. Then, after a brief period as a belle, she married the Creole Oscar Chopin when she was nineteen. For ten years they lived in New Orleans, where he was a cotton factor, and then, from 1880 to his death in 1882, at the McAlpin Plantation in Cloutierville, which he managed for his family. After he died, his widow managed the plantation for a year before moving back to Saint Louis in 1883 with her six children. A woman of comfortable leisure, Kate Chopin had perfected her French in Louisiana, and the reading which prompted her to attempt writing fiction was chiefly in that language. Her admiration for Maupassant especially inspired her to try short stories. For eleven years, through 1898, she wrote poems, criticisms, and a play, but concentrated mainly on two novels and about one hundred short stories, almost all of which are set among the Creoles in Nachitoches Parish. The first of her novels, *At Fault* (1890), was not read; and, stung by its failure, she was so critical of her second novel that she destroyed it. But her stories were given a modestly warm reception.

The most popular of Mrs. Chopin's stories, while they make full use of the charming lilt of Creole English and the easy openness of Creole manners, concern themselves, as do Maupassant's, with some central quirk or turn in

---

From *The American 1890's: Life and Times of a Lost Generation.* © 1966 by Larzer Ziff. Viking, 1966.

events which reverses the situation that was initially presented. In "Désirée's Baby" Désirée commits infanticide and suicide when her infant shows increasing signs of being partly Negro; she, a foundling, assumes that she has brought this shame on her proud Creole husband. After the deaths, however, the husband, who is not entirely unhappy at the convenient removal of his difficulties, discovers that it is he, not Désirée, who has Negro blood. So, characteristically, does the Chopin story depend on a twist.

But more important to Kate Chopin's art than such plotting was her acceptance of the Creole outlook as the ambiance of her tales. The community about which she wrote was one in which respectable women took wine with their dinner and brandy after it, smoked cigarettes, played Chopin sonatas, and listened to the men tell risqué stories. It was, in short, far more French than American, and Mrs. Chopin reproduced this little world with no specific intent to shock or make a point, as did, for instance, Frederic, who was straining after a specific effect when he posed his Celia Madden at the piano with a cigarette. Rather, these were for Mrs. Chopin the conditions of civility, and, since they were so French, a magazine public accustomed to accepting naughtiness from that quarter and taking pleasure in it on those terms raised no protest. But for Mrs. Chopin they were only outward signs of a culture that was hers and had its inner effects in the moral make-up of her characters. Though she seldom turned her plot on these facts, she showed that her women were capable of loving more than one man at a time and were not only attractive but sexually attracted also.

The quality of daily life in Kate Chopin's Natchitoches is genial and kind. People openly like one another, enjoy life, and savor its sensual riches. Their likes and their dislikes are held passionately, so that action bears a close and apparent relation to feeling. In setting a character, Mrs. Chopin writes, "Grégoire loved women. He liked their nearness, their atmosphere; the tones of their voices and the things they said; their ways of moving and turning about; the brushing of their garments when they passed him by pleased him." This open delight in the difference between the sexes was not a mentionable feeling until Mrs. Chopin brought to American literature a setting in which it could be demonstrated with an open geniality.

In almost all her stories, however, Kate Chopin conventionalized the activities of her passionate characters, and even in some cases betrayed them for the sake of exploiting the quaintness of it all. The ambiance of sensuality was rarely permitted to permeate the actions on which the stories turned. But she was obviously growing in that direction. In "Athénaise" she told the story of a romantic goose of a girl who married too soon and, encouraged by a brother with a flair for melodrama, left her husband's plantation to hide in New Orleans for no other reason than that she was not prepared to accept the anti-romantic termination of her youthful yearnings that marriage represented. She came near having an affair in New Orleans, but then, discovering that she was carrying her husband's baby, she returned to him. Thus summarized, the plot, while slightly daring, ends conventionally enough. Mrs. Chopin, however, does not accept the justification which convention would give her ending, but indicates that if the girl returns to her husband because she is pregnant, it is not merely to have a child in a respectable fashion but also because her pregnancy has, biologically as well as mentally, converted her into a woman, and she now feels passionately toward the man with whom she lives. Just as marriage was not a termination for Athénaise, neither, the reader gathers, will childbirth be. The story is a fragment of life; the wife will go on growing in her attempts to discover her nature and may very well, at a later date, meet somebody else in New Orleans. But the return to home and husband is all Mrs. Chopin here permits herself.

In her unsuccessful first novel, *At Fault,* Kate Chopin used the successive-marriage plot in a rather wooden fashion to explore the responsibilities of the sexes toward each other, and it contains little that should have made it a success. She was trying her hand at full-length works too soon after beginning to write, and her characters refuse to take on the life she learned to give them after a longer apprenticeship in story-writing. The novel is critical of the dependence of either sex upon the other—a woman is dependent upon a man, her husband, who in turn is dependent upon another woman, whom he will eventually marry—and finds both the married woman who is kept in a tidy home by her husband and the new independent woman who duels with her suitors unacceptable. The first passes her time in petty card playing and in idle gossip; the second flirts aimlessly between attendance at such functions as "An Hour with Hegel" or a meeting of the Hospital Society. The admirable woman, presumably, is the widow who is successfully managing a plantation; she is making sensible use of her independence but nevertheless recognizes her sexual need for a man, while enjoying the self-sufficiency that will allow her to make a choice on her terms. The novel, however, proceeds by contrivance rather than psychological analysis, and, since the theme is the nature of self-fulfillment, analysis is urgently needed.

The stories Kate Chopin wrote after she destroyed her second novel showed an increasing deftness of style and a greater daring in relating the open sensuality of her characters to their inner cravings and their actions. But the editorial policy of the magazines to which she contributed would not have permitted her a full exploration of such themes, so that, after ten years of writing, she again turned to the novel form to bring together the

Creole environment and the theme of feminine self-awareness which she had approached tangentially in *At Fault* and stories such as "Athénaise." The result was *The Awakening* (1899), a novel of the first rank.

Like *Madame Bovary, The Awakening* is about the adulterous experiments of a married woman, and while Mrs. Chopin did not have to go to Flaubert for the theme, she obviously was indebted to him for it as well as for the masterful economy of setting and character and the precision of style which she here achieved. Sarah Orne Jewett had also been an admirer of *Madame Bovary* and had defended Flaubert's theme by saying that "a master writer gives everything weight." But she had drawn quite a different moral from the novel. Miss Jewett wrote of Emma Bovary: "She is such a lesson to dwellers in country towns, who drift out of relation to their surroundings, not only social, but the very companionship of nature, unknown to them." Emma Bovary is a foolish, bored woman, while Mrs. Chopin's Edna Pontellier is an intelligent, nervous woman, but Edna's salvation is not to be found in drifting back into relation with her environment. Rather, the questions Mrs. Chopin raises through her are what sort of nature she, twenty-eight years of age, married to a rich man and the mother of two children, possesses, and how her life is related to the dynamics of her inner self. Sarah Jewett counseled sublimation; Kate Chopin pursued self-discovery and counseled not at all.

The novel opens at Grand Isle in the Gulf of Mexico, where Edna and her children are spending the summer in a cottage at a resort managed by the LeBrun family. She is surrounded by other well-to-do women with their families, all of whom spend their languorous days in expectation of, and in resting after, the weekend visits of the husbands, who work in New Orleans. In and out of the field of vision tortured by the constant glare of the sun pass the mothers and their children, a lady in black, solitary and always at her beads, and a pair of young lovers. They suggest the horizons of experience. But there is also the sea:

> The voice of the sea is seductive; never ceasing, whispering, clamoring, murmuring, inviting the soul to wander for a spell in abysses of solitude; to lose itself in mazes of inward contemplation.
> The voice of the sea speaks to the soul. The touch of the sea is sensuous, enfolding the body in its soft, close embrace.

The vague suggestions of the sea keep alive in Edna the questions which have forced themselves unwelcomed upon her. She is the wife of a man who loves her and whom she likes and respects. He cares for her fully and handsomely and leaves her with no sound reason for the discontent she feels now when her nature, like something awakening, yearns for some greater fulfillment and tells her that in her husband and children she has assumed a responsibility for which she was not fitted.

The sea reminds her of the sea of grass in Kentucky, where she was born and raised. There at the age of ten she had fancied herself in love with a passing cavalry officer and had indulged in fantasies about him, fantasies so intense that her father's reading of Presbyterian family prayers threatened the romantic childish self she had constructed and, on one memorable day, she ran from the call to prayers in a long flight which led her swimming deeper and deeper into the sea of grass in protection of her infantile passion. Edna as a girl dreamed of men, and she married Léonce Pontellier because he was devoted to her and because her father violently opposed the marriage, Léonce being a Catholic.

Now, at Grand Isle, her Kentucky background, warring with her unfulfilled fantasies, still makes her uneasy with the Creole life to which she is also attracted:

> The mother-women seemed to prevail that summer at Grand Isle. It was easy to know them, fluttering about with extended, protecting wings when any harm, real or imaginary, threatened their precious brood. They were women who idolized their children, worshipped their husbands, and esteemed it a holy privilege to efface themselves as individuals and grow wings as ministering angels.

Edna refuses to acknowledge her membership in this group, and yet it is not because the group is smug or contented. Quite the contrary; their mature and easy attitude toward the experiences they have shared goes against something of her father in her:

> A characteristic which distinguished them and which impressed Mrs. Pontellier most forcibly was their entire absence of prudery. Their freedom of expression was at first incomprehensible to her, though she had no difficulty in reconciling it with a lofty chastity which in the Creole woman seems to be inborn and unmistakable.

She is secretly disturbed at the detail in which the women discuss their *accouchements,* the books they read, the droll stories the men tell them. She wants a fulfillment greater than the motherhood they have accepted, and yet she is more prudish than they in the face of sexual experience because her own background has made it a thing more personal.

At one point Edna attempts to explain to Adèle, a strikingly beautiful woman and the devoted mother of a flock of children, what she feels toward her two sons. She says, "I would give up the unessential; I would give my money, I would give my life for my children; but I wouldn't give myself. I can't make it more clear; it's only something which I am beginning to comprehend, which is revealing itself to me." Adèle doesn't understand her but approvingly notes that she could hardly give more than her life for her children, and Edna, uncertain as to whether she understands her awakening self either, laughs.

The vague yearnings Edna feels fix on Robert LeBrun, a young and handsome Creole; however, when he feels the attraction of Edna, he responds by accepting employment out of the country so as to preserve the code of chastity to which he assumes she, like other women of his class, is committed. After the vacation season Edna returns to the family home in New Orleans, restless and frustrated, feeling she has yet to realize herself. Her fantasies are dominated by the figure of a naked man standing in hopeless resignation by a rock on the seashore. Léonce Pontellier, sympathetically noticing that his wife is not herself, indulges her as best he can, but to the phrase "she is not herself," Mrs. Chopin adds, "That is, he could not see that she was becoming herself and daily casting aside that fictitious self which we assume like a garment with which to appear before the world."

In New Orleans in the winter Edna's awakening nature strongly turns to sexual desire as she dotes on the memory of Robert LeBrun, and in his absence she allows herself to drift into an affair with Alcée Arobin, a pleasant rake who is one of the few men of her class willing to put aside the code of chastity that surrounds Creole women; besides, he rationalizes, Edna is not really a Creole. The affair is consummated without any great shame on Edna's part, but her distress quickens at the realization that Arobin does not satisfy her and that her nature still calls for more from life.

At this juncture young LeBrun returns from abroad, and when he visits her at her home she forces him to speak of his love for her. But her impetuous forcing of their meeting to a sexual conclusion is interrupted by a call for her to attend Adèle in childbirth, and she leaves LeBrun to await her return. At Adèle's bedside her obligations as a "mother-woman" flood in upon her, but the thought of Robert waiting for her is sufficient to dam them. When she returns home to find he has left, however, because, as his note explains, he loves her and therefore dares not destroy her life, she is brought to the realization that she is on the brink of a series of lovers: "To-day it is Arobin; to-morrow it will be some one else." It makes no difference to her, and she doesn't feel her husband really matters, but the effect of her affairs on her children frightens her. "The children appeared before her," says Mrs. Chopin, "like antagonists who had overcome her; who had overpowered and sought to drag her into the soul's slavery for the rest of her days." For their sake only she must accept marriage as the termination of her development and must arrest her awakening.

Edna, however, refuses to do this. She fully realizes for the first time what she meant when she said she would give everything for her children, even life, but she would not give herself. On a spring morning before the vacationers have returned, she appears at Grand Isle, leaves her clothing on the beach, and, naked, swims out to give herself to the sea.

The Awakening was the most important piece of fiction about the sexual life of a woman written to date in America, and the first fully to face the fact that marriage, whether in point of fact it closed the range of a woman's sexual experiences or not, was but an episode in her continuous growth. It did not attack the institution of the family, but it rejected the family as the automatic equivalent of feminine self-fulfillment, and on the very eve of the twentieth century it raised the question of what woman was to do with the freedom she struggled toward. The Creole woman's acceptance of maternity as totally adequate to the capacities of her nature carried with it the complements of a fierce chastity, a frankness of speech on sexual matters, a mature ease among men, and a frank and unguilty pleasure in sensual indulgence. But this was not, ultimately, Edna Pontellier's birthright, and she knew it. She was an American woman, raised in the Protestant mistrust of the senses and in the detestation of sexual desire as the root of evil. As a result, the hidden act came for her to be equivalent to the hidden and the true self, once her nature awakened in the open surroundings of Creole Louisiana. The new century was to provide just such an awakening for countless American women, and *The Awakening* spoke of painful times ahead on the road to fulfillment.

Kate Chopin sympathized with Edna, but she did not pity her. She rendered her story with a detachment akin to Flaubert's. At one point Edna's doctor says, "Youth is given up to illusions. It seems to be a provision of Nature; a decoy to secure mothers for the race. And Nature takes no account of moral consequences, of arbitrary conditions which we create, and which we feel obliged to maintain at any cost." These appear to be the author's sentiments. Edna Pontellier is trapped between her illusions and the conditions which society arbitrarily establishes to maintain itself, and she is made to pay. Whether girls should be educated free of illusions, if possible, whether society should change the conditions it imposes on women, or whether both are needed, the author does not say; the novel is about what happened to Edna Pontellier.

The Awakening was published by Herbert S. Stone, who had gone on from his partnership with Kimball and the publication of *The Chap-Book* to establish his own house, where he maintained an active interest in uncovering new talent and printing experimental work. The reviews it received, however, were firm in their rejection of Mrs. Chopin's topic. In her own city of St. Louis the libaries refused to circulate the book, and the Fine Arts Club denied her membership because of it. Kate Chopin was not merely rejected; she was insulted. "She was broken-hearted," her son Felix said, and in the remaining five years of her life she produced only a few pieces, although her friends insisted that she still had a great deal to say.

Kate Chopin, a wise and worldly woman, had refined the craft of fiction in the nineties to the point where it could face her strong inner theme of the female rebellion and see it through to a superb creative work. *The Awakening* was also an awakening of the deepest powers in its author, but, like Edna Pontellier, Kate Chopin learned that her society would not tolerate her questioning. Her tortured silence as the new century arrived was a loss to American letters of the order of the untimely deaths of Crane and Norris. She was alive when the twentieth century began, but she had been struck mute by a society fearful in the face of an uncertain dawn.

DONALD A. RINGE

Cane River World:
At Fault *and Related Stories*

Because of the growing interest in Kate Chopin's *The Awakening* over the last twenty years, critical attention has slowly been drawn to the fiction she had written before the appearance of that book. Though one may rejoice that the whole of Chopin's work is at last becoming more widely known, the process of her rediscovery has turned into some unpromising channels. Because *The Awakening* is so powerful a book, the temptation has been strong to read *At Fault,* her first novel, in terms of the later and better known one, and to value most highly those stories in which the theme of female emancipation is adumbrated. To follow this line of approach, however, the critic must assume a thematic development in Chopin's fiction which may not actually be present. Hence, he courts the danger of misinterpreting a work that falls outside the pattern his critical predilections have led him to expect. A second line of inquiry has correctly recognized the theme of social change in *At Fault,* but, reading back from the novels of William Faulkner, has seen in the book a secondary theme of "Southern racial guilt" derived from slavery. The concerns of a twentieth-century novelist are thus used to interpret a nineteenth-century one.

But when Kate Chopin wrote *At Fault* and her first Creole stories, she could not have known where her literary career would eventually take her, nor is it likely that she began to write with the purpose of developing throughout her work the theme which critics see in *The Awakening*. Though

From *Studies in American Fiction* 3, no. 2 (Autumn 1975). © 1975 by Northeastern University.

a few of her early stories do indeed point in this direction, *At Fault* and the stories related to it in character and setting bear little relation to that theme. A novice at writing fiction, Chopin seems, rather, to have drawn freely upon her own experience in Natchitoches Parish to develop in her earliest fiction a picture of the social world of northwest Louisiana in the years immediately following the Civil War and Reconstruction. These were years, as everyone knows, of great social change, much of which is either hinted at or assumed in Chopin's early fiction, but it is not a period in which one might expect to find a strong sense of racial guilt or an attempt to embody it in fiction. It would seem more reasonable, therefore, to lay aside all preconceptions and begin with an analysis of the social world she actually depicts, the Cane River country of Louisiana in the post-Reconstruction period.

This is not to say that the early fiction of Kate Chopin treats the social issues to be found, for example, in so strong a novel of the New South as George Washington Cable's *John March, Southerner,* where the problems of a reconstructed society are clearly paramount. Such was not her purpose. But neither did she ignore the social and historical realities of her Cane River world. If *At Fault* is read in conjunction with those stories that are closely related to it, there emerges a fictive world with a considerable amount of social and historical density. The action of *At Fault,* for example, can be very precisely dated. In the opening chapter of the novel, a railroad is constructed that causes Thérèse, the widow of Jérôme Lafirme, to move her house. The time, therefore, is 1881, the year the Texas and Pacific Railroad was built in Natchitoches Parish. The Civil War has been over for some sixteen years, and Reconstruction had ended with the removal of Federal troops in 1877. Both of these events are far enough in the past to have ceased being topics of conversation—and indeed neither is mentioned in the book—but the war itself, Chopin makes clear in her stories, has had its effect on the society she depicts.

Several of the stories Chopin wrote after she published *At Fault* give the historical background. The effects of the war in Natchitoches Parish were varied. The home of Ma'ame Pélagie on Côte Joyeuse, "a region of large cotton plantations" on Cane River, was burned by Federal troops, and many years later, she recalls among the ruins how young Jérôme Lafirme and the Santien family had once been guests in it. The Santiens themselves had been all but destroyed by the conflict. Old Lucien Santien had owned a hundred slaves and a thousand acres on Red River, but after the war, his son Jules "was not the man to mend such damage as the war had left," and his three sons, Hector, Grégoire, and Placide, were even less able than he to retrieve the loss. Hence, the Santien land has passed out of the family. Joe Duplan, on the other hand, who served in the Civil War with the Louisiana Tigers, had managed to keep his plantation, Les Chênieres, and he still works it profitably many years after the war is over. Jérôme Lafirme must also have been successful since there is no mention in Chopin's works of any loss he had suffered.

What makes this history important is that Thérèse is involved with many of these people. She married Jérôme Lafirme and counts among her friends Joe Duplan and his wife. Even more to the point, she must herself have been a Santien before she was married. Since Grégoire Santien is her nephew, and his mother was a French woman who eventually returned to her native country, Thérèse must be the sister of Jules Santien and the daughter of old Lucien. Her black nurse, moreover, Marie Louise, "the only one of the family servants who had come with her mistress from New Orleans to Place-du-Bois at that lady's marriage," had learned to cook under the instruction of Lucien Santien, a famed gourmet. Though Thérèse was only a girl during the war (she must have been born in 1851 since she is thirty when the novel begins), her personal history has been strongly affected by that conflict. She is, however, a stronger person than any of her male relatives, and she faces adversity more courageously. When her husband dies, she soon recovers her equanimity, learns to manage her plantation, and achieves a very practical success.

Not all the people of Cane River, of course, belong to this class. Some of the stories deal with the poorer ones who live on the Rigolet de Bon Dieu, and the free mulattoes—those who were never enslaved—who inhabit l'Isle de Mulatres. There are skilled workers like the carpenter Azenor in "Love on the Bon Dieu" and even a misanthrope, M'sieur Michel, who, returning from the war to find his children dead and his wife run off with another man, lives alone in the woods until retrieved at last by Joe Duplan. None of this appears, of course, in *At Fault,* but Chopin does include the half-Indian Joçint and his black father, Morico, as well as assorted black people of varying dispositions: both the faithful nurse, Marie Louise, and the hard-working Aunt Belindy, who mutters to herself about the white folks' lack of feeling when they delay coming to supper and make her work more difficult. There are even the blacks who manage skillfully to evade the domestic service they do not wish to perform without offending their masters. They seem to accept the proffered jobs and escape with vague excuses for not having shown up to work.

Taken in the aggregate, Kate Chopin's Cane River world is a coherent one, well located in both time and space, and containing a richness and density that are well worthy of note. Had Chopin managed to get the whole of it into *At Fault,* she might have written as fine a novel as Cable's *Gran-*

dissimes and might even have foreshadowed Faulkner's Yoknapatawpha more clearly than she does. But because *At Fault* is among her earliest work, it exhibits some of the thinness and lack of control of a first novel, and the full development of the material had to wait until the stories that immediately followed it. The picture of the society, therefore, is necessarily fragmented. The consistency of its development throughout her stories, however, suggests that it may well have been firmly in her mind from the beginning of her career, and a knowledge of it throws considerable light on her first novel. To a very great extent, *At Fault* is a book about the changing social world of the post-Reconstruction South and its effects on the people who inhabit it.

The major change, of course, is the intrusion of modern industry into the agricultural world of the plantation. The book begins with the arrival of the railroad at Place-du-Bois, the removal to the new farmhouse, and the intrusion of the "brown and ugly" station into Thérèse's "fair domain." With the railroad comes the sawmill and David Hosmer, a businessman from St. Louis, whose face reveals "a too close attention to what men are pleased to call the main chances of life," and who resists all hospitality in his desire to be about his business. Progressive civilization has arrived in the Cane River world with a lure that even Thérèse, in her reluctance to accept change, cannot resist. Hosmer offers her a large sum of money "for the privilege of cutting timber from her land for a given number of years." A shrewd businesswoman, Thérèse asks for time to consider the proposal before she makes up her mind, but the issue is never really in doubt. As soon as Hosmer leaves, Thérèse goes "out to her beloved woods, and at the hush of mid-day, [bids] a tearful farewell to the silence." The changes set in motion by this decision have a number of far-reaching results.

As might be expected, the vestiges of the past are totally destroyed by the advent of the new. Joçint, for example, whose Indian blood and love of hunting bespeak the dislocation that occurred when the land was originally settled, deeply resents the new intrusion. Though the free life of the woods alone appeals to the young man, he is forced by his father to work in the sawmill that David Hosmer constructs. There is irony in the fact that Joçint is not only prevented from living his carefree life but is even forced to cut into lumber the very woods where he loves to hunt, in effect destroying the thing that means most to him. It is small wonder, then, that Joçint gets repeatedly into trouble and eventually plans to burn the mill. On Halloween, when all the blacks stay in their cabins in superstitious fear, and the land seems all but deserted, Joçint pours kerosene on the mill and sets it afire. Such a protest against change is, of course, futile, and Joçint is shot dead by Grégoire Santien, who catches him in the act of arson. With Joçint's death, the primitive past is dismissed, the mill is rebuilt, and change continues on Place-du-Bois.

Yet Grégoire is as out of place as Joçint in the new industrial world. Like the Indian boy, he is thoroughly at ease in traversing the swamp, yet he shares with the blacks some of the superstitious fear of ghosts they exhibit. His background, moreover, has largely unfitted him for the new environment. The scion of wealthy slaveholders and a man who has always done pretty much as he pleased, Grégoire has felt few restraints. The family plantation lost because of the Civil War and the ineptitude of his father, Grégoire, like his brothers, Hector and Placide, has shown himself unable to meet the vicissitudes of his fortune. Each of the three, as is revealed in several stories, has slipped to a lower level of society, and all that remains of their family past is the chivalric attitude that each has retained toward women. Grégoire himself falls in love with Mélicent Hosmer, David's sister, but the love affair ends unhappily. When Grégoire, with primitive directness, shoots down the unarmed Joçint, Mélicent is so repulsed that she will have nothing more to do with him. In a state of despair, Grégoire departs for Texas, where he is himself gunned down in an altercation with a man who scornfully calls him "Frenchy."

Joçint and Grégoire cannot adjust to a changing world: their inner natures simply will not permit it. Joçint cannot both remain himself and work at the mill, and though Grégoire tries to become something other than what he has been, he is finally unsuccessful. A completely undisciplined hell-raiser in his early youth, Grégoire seems to change when he falls in love with Mélicent. As Aunt Belindy tells her, "God! but dats a diffunt man sence you come heah. . . . 'f you warn't heah dat same Mista Grégor 'd be in Centaville ev'y Sunday, a raisin' Cain. Humph—I knows 'im." Mélicent herself has perceived that Grégoire has "always been more or less under restraint with her," and she would like "to get at the truth concerning him." That truth is revealed not only in his killing of Joçint, but also in the way he reacts when Mélicent rejects him: he reverts to his former habits of "raisin' Cain." Grégoire becomes once again his unrestrained self, a matter of no surprise to Aunt Belindy, who, when she hears of one of his escapades in town, tells Uncle Hiram, "Don't you know Grégor gwine be Grégor tell he die? Dat's all dar is 'bout it."

The rejection and death of Grégoire leaves unresolved the question of whether he could have changed as a consequence of his love. Grégoire, it could be argued, returns to his earlier ways only because Mélicent cannot accept him as he is, with all the potentiality for violence that lies at the heart of his nature. Had she responded to his passion, Grégoire might conceivably

have become a different person. Such a conjecture is idle, however, for Mélicent is not that kind of woman. Her response to him is feeble, as it has been
apparently to other men who have loved her. Unstable, capricious, indeed
rather cold in her relations with others, Mélicent has gone wherever her
whim has taken her and shifts her interests as new attractions catch her eye.
Incapable of forming the kind of lasting relationship that Grégoire's love
demands, she holds herself aloof from him as long as he lives. It is only after
his death that she can respond with warmth to the one kiss he had given
her, and though she goes into mourning for him, she is simply playing a role
that will keep her from boredom until a new interest attracts her attention,
as one soon does.

The action of the novel clearly implies that change is not to be looked
for in these characters. Each is, in a sense, the prisoner of his inner self and
acts out the life that his nature demands. In one way or another, Joçint must
be destroyed by the mill, Grégoire must live and die by unrestrained violence,
and Mélicent must drift aimlessly with the times. Their fates contain, moreover, certain implications for the Cane River world they inhabit. By their
violent deaths, Joçint and Grégoire suggest the passing of the older worlds
that formed their lives, and Mélicent's rootless wandering clearly implies that
the northern, urban world from which she comes holds little hope for the
future. Seen in these terms, the love affair of Mélicent and Grégoire must
come to nought. The union of new and old, urban and rural, North and
South cannot be accomplished through them. Grégoire contains perhaps too
much of the past for him to bridge easily the gulf that separates it from the
present, and she is so lacking in any true sense of identity or commitment
that she cannot lead him into a modern world of form and substance.

Thérèse Lafirme and David Hosmer, on the other hand, can perform
the function that lies beyond the capabilities of Mélicent and Grégoire. Unlike her nephew, Thérèse has already made an important adjustment to
change when the story opens. She learns to run her plantation successfully
in the post-Reconstruction age and accepts the business and industrial development that comes with the sawmill. David, on his part, has escaped from
an unfortunate marriage, and, leaving behind the world of St. Louis where
he had lived with Fanny, his former wife, he is able to devote himself to the
business interests that have always absorbed his attention. Both may be seen
as turning away from the past and moving forward into a future for which
each appears to be well prepared. Once they discover their mutual love,
moreover, the union of old and new would seem to be imminent. At this
point, however, Thérèse learns for the first time that David has been divorced,
and she not only refuses to marry him while his former wife still lives, but

even demands that he remarry her. When David accedes to her wishes, their union and all that it might represent is thwarted.

The cause of the trouble lies, once again, in the characters themselves. Secure in her Cane River world, Thérèse Lafirme acts like a benevolent despot, ruling her plantation with such gentle force that almost everyone at Place-du-Bois has felt the influence of her exacting nature. Not that Thérèse is imperious in her demands. If others must conduct themselves as she wills, she brings about the result through personal efforts of her own that leave no doubt in anyone's mind "of the pure unselfishness of her motive." Thérèse never seems to realize, however, that in making her demands, she not only restricts the freedom of others to do as they will, but even courts the danger of violating their integrity. Thérèse may refuse to marry David for whatever reasons she may have, but she does not have the right to take the fate of David and Fanny Hosmer into her own hands. In doing so, she forces them back into a life that had lost all meaning for them, yet one to which they cannot really return. David's experience at Place-du-Bois and his love for Thérèse are unalterable conditions that make his new life with Fanny more miserable than his former one.

That life had been bad enough. A modern, rootless urbanite, Fanny Larimore had lived in an empty world well characterized by her St. Louis friends. Belle Worthington and Lou Dawson are "two ladies of elegant leisure, the conditions of whose lives, and the amiability of whose husbands, had enabled them to develop into finished and professional time-killers." Mindless matinee-goers, they care little for anyone but themselves. Belle Worthington, a domineering woman, has only contempt for the small, bookish man she married, and Lou Dawson, something of a flirt, eventually becomes involved with another man when she thinks her traveling-salesman husband is out of town. These women comprise the society in which Fanny wants to move, but which David found so distasteful when he first lived with her in St. Louis. Yet if David abhors the kind of life that Fanny prefers, she dislikes the plantation world to which David takes her after their remarriage. Fanny is unhappy in her new environment. Even without the knowledge of David's love for Thérèse, her life is utterly miserable and she turns to drink to endure it. With that awareness, it becomes completely unbearable.

Caught in the same impasse is David Hosmer. The victim, to some extent, of his single-minded pursuit of business success, he has never formed the proper kind of human attachment nor developed the moral perception he needs. Too easily attracted to Fanny when he first met her, he is also too easily influenced by Thérèse. Though well aware of her penchant for meddling in the lives of others, he nonetheless submits to her judgment that he remarry his former wife. David's love for Thérèse, his belief in her moral superiority, and a twinge of conscience which tells him that he had not been entirely fair to Fanny during their marriage influence his decision. By acting upon the moral judgment of another, however, David becomes false to his own inner nature. He returns to a life he abhors, made all the more horrid and sickening by his thwarted love for Thérèse. That the marriage lasts at all results from an act of will. He forces himself to play a role that is false—to be good to a wife he has come to hate—and he suffers severely under the strain he must endure.

Because of Thérèse's meddling, Place-du-Bois, which once held out the hope for a better future, becomes a place of unrelieved misery. David simply braces himself to endure, Fanny continues to drink, and Thérèse begins to doubt the wisdom of her decisions. Though she never fully knows the misery that David and Fanny experience, she sees enough to ask herself if she had been right in the choice she had forced upon him. Their acts and her doubts avail nothing, however. It takes a natural disaster to break the impasse and set the current of change once again in the right direction. Her supply of whisky cut off by the absence of Sampson, the small black boy who supplies her, Fanny goes out in a storm in search of him, crosses the swollen river, and, successful in her quest, rests in the cabin of Marie Louise perched high on the bank above the water. When David catches up with her, she, half-drunk, refuses to go home with him, and as he recrosses the stream, the bank collapses. Although David tries valiantly to save her, Fanny drowns when the shack falls into the water.

Such a solution to the problem of the three main characters has, of course, been criticized as a weakness in the novel, for it seems to be only a mechanical means for providing the happy ending that Chopin seems to have sought. Yet, unfortunate though the device may be, it serves nonetheless an important thematic function. As Thérèse Lafirme's old nurse, Marie Louise lives apart from the other servants, and although her cabin has previously been moved out of danger from the river, she resists any further removals, even though the stream once again poses a threat to it. Her refusal to change is thus the ultimate cause of the disaster in which both she and Fanny Hosmer meet their deaths. Since Grégoire is already dead and Mélicent has gone off to lead her own aimless life, Marie Louise and Fanny represent the last links to the past of the two main characters: the one to Thérèse's Santien girlhood, the other to the St. Louis world that David has sought to escape from. Their deaths in the river may be seen as a final symbolic freeing of Thérèse and David from their former selves. Henceforth, they will be free to move forward together.

When Thérèse and David marry, the potential for change in the Cane River world can at last be fulfilled. The past is gone. Joçint, Grégoire, Marie Louise, and Fanny are all dead. And the rootless urban world of which Mélicent writes in her letters seems as far removed from Place-du-Bois as the scandal she relates about Fanny's St. Louis friends. Both Thérèse and David have changed, but neither has lost the best of their former worlds. Thérèse still runs the plantation, but, with a new sense of humility, she no longer feels so secure in her own perception of right. David, on his part, still runs the mill—indeed, he plans to expand it—but he no longer has the obsession for business that characterized him on his initial visit to Place-du-Bois. He thinks, rather, that, through division of labor, the expanded mill will give him more time for Thérèse, and he finds a new strength and courage in her love. In Thérèse and David, therefore, rural and urban meet, South and North become one, and the Cane River past flows into a future that is filled with promise.

CYNTHIA GRIFFIN WOLFF

The Fiction of Limits:
"Désirée's Baby"

For many years, "Désirée's Baby" was the one piece of Chopin's fiction most likely to be known; even today, despite the wide respect that her second novel has won, there are still readers whose acquaintance with Chopin's work is restricted to this one, widely-anthologized short story. Rankin, who did not feel the need to reprint "Désirée's Baby" in *Kate Chopin and Her Creole Tales,* nonetheless judged it "perhaps . . . one of the world's best short stories." Unfortunately, Rankin left future critics a terminology with which to describe the value of this and other studies in *Bayou Folk:* it had the "freshness which springs from an unexplored field—the quaint and pictur-esque life among the Creole and Acadian folk of the Louisiana bayous." In short, it was excellent "regional" work—hence limited to certain circum-scribed triumphs.

Critics' tendency to dismiss Chopin's fiction as little more than local color began to diminish by the late 1950s; nevertheless, old habits died hard. "Désirée's Baby" continued to be the most frequently anthologized of her short fictions, and while the comments on it strained after some larger tragic significance, the definition of that "tragedy" was still formulated almost exclusively in "regional" terms. Claude M. Simpson introduces the tale in his collection with a brief essay on the local color movement and concludes that the story draws its effect from a reader's appreciation of the impartial cruelties of the slave system. Several years later, in another anthology of

From *Southern Literary Journal* 10, no. 2 (Spring 1978). © 1978 by the Department of English of the University of North Carolina at Chapel Hill.

American short stories, Eugene Current-Garcia and Walton R. Patrick give Chopin credit (again as a regionalist) for daring to touch upon the forbidden subject of miscegenation; and, of course, the story they select to illustrate Chopin's particular talent is "Désirée's Baby."

Other critics, still acknowledging the importance of regional elements in the tale, seek to discover the reasons for its persistently compelling quality by examining the structure. Thus Larzer Ziff observes that "the most popular of Mrs. Chopin's stories, while they make full use of the charming lilt of Creole English and the easy openness of Creole manners, concern themselves, as do Maupassant's, with some central quirk or turn in events which reverses the situation that was initially presented." He cites the conclusion of "Désirée's Baby" as an example: "So, characteristically, does the Chopin story depend on a twist." Taking a similar view, Per Seyersted remarks the "taut compression and restrained intensity" of the tale and then notes (with some asperity) that "the surprise ending, though somewhat contrived, has a bitter, piercing quality that could not have been surpassed by [Maupassant] himself." Yet, in the final analysis, these judgments are no more satisfactory than those that grow from the more narrow definition of Chopin as "local colorist": if significant effects are seldom achieved merely through a deft management of dialect and scenery, it is also the case that a "trick" or "surprise" conclusion is almost never a sufficient means by which to evoke a powerful and poignant reaction from the reader.

Thus "Désirée's Baby" remains an enigma. We still tend to admire it and to demonstrate our admiration by selecting it to appear in anthologies; yet the admiration is given somewhat grudgingly—perhaps because we cannot fully comprehend the story. The specifically Southern elements of the story seem significant; however, the nature of their force is not clear. The reversal of the situation that concludes the tale is important (although to a discerning reader it may well be no surprise), but, contrary to Seyersted's remarks, the story's full impact patently does not derive from this writer's "trick." And while the story has been accepted as characteristic of Chopin's work, it is in several ways unusual or unique—being the only one of her fictions to touch upon the subject of miscegenation, for example. We might respond to this accumulation of contradictions by assuming that a mistake has been made somewhere along the line—that the tale has been misinterpreted or that it is not really representative of Chopin's fiction. Yet such an assumption would not explain the force of those many years of readers' response; in the end, it would not resolve the persistent enigma of "Désirée's Baby." Alternatively, we might try to understand why critics' judgments of the story have been so different, presuming such judgments to be insufficient but not, perhaps, fundamentally incorrect. But more importantly, we must expand our vision of the story in order to see precisely those ways in which it articulates and develops themes that are central to other of Chopin's works.

A majority of Chopin's fictions are set in worlds where stability or permanence is a precarious state: change is always threatened—by the vagaries of impassive fate, by the assaults of potentially ungovernable individual passions, or merely by the inexorable passage of time. More generally, we might say that Chopin construes existence as necessarily uncertain. By definition, then, to live is to be vulnerable; and the artist who would capture the essence of life will turn his attention to those intimate and timeless moments when the comforting illusion of certainty is unbalanced by those forces that may disrupt and destroy. Insofar as Chopin can be said to emulate Maupassant, who stands virtually alone as her avowed literary model, we might say that she strives to look "out upon life through [her] own being and with [her] own eyes"; that she desires no more than to tell us what she sees "in a direct and simple way." Nor is Chopin's vision dissimilar to Maupassant's, for what she sees is the ominous and insistent presence of the margin: the inescapable fact that even our most vital moments must be experienced on the boundary—always threatening to slip away from us into something else, into some dark, undefined contingency. The careful exploration of this bourne is, in some sense, then, the true subject for much of her best fiction.

Certainly it is the core subject of "Désirée's Baby"—a story that treats layers of ambiguity and uncertainty with ruthless economy. Indeed, the tale is almost a paradigmatic study of the demarcating limits of human experience, and—since this subject is so typically the center of Chopin's attention—our continuing intuition that this story is a quite appropriate selection to stand as "representative" of her work must be seen as fundamentally correct. What is more, if we understand the true focus of this fiction, we are also in a position to comprehend the success of its conclusion. The "twist" is no mere writer's trick; rather, it is the natural consequence—one might say the necessary and inevitable concomitant—of life as Chopin construes it.

At the most superficial level in "Désirée's Baby," there are distinctions that attend coloration, differences of pigment that carry definitions of social caste and even more damning implications about the "value" of one's "identity." The problem of race is managed quite idiosyncratically in this tale: we have already noted that this is the only one of Chopin's many stories to treat miscegenation directly or explicitly; however, we can be ever more emphatic—this is the only story even to probe the implications of those many hues of skin that were deemed to comprise the "negro" population. Yet from the very beginning Chopin focuses our attention upon this element with inescapable determination: she chooses not to use dialect conversation; she reduces the description of architecture and vegetation to a minimum—leaving only the thematically necessary elements. The result is a tale where the differences between "black" and "white" remain as the only way to locate the events—its only "regional" aspects, if you will—and we cannot avoid attending to them.

Yet for all this artistic direction, Chopin is clearly not primarily interested in dissecting the *social problem* of slavery (as Cable might be); rather, she limits herself almost entirely to the personal and the interior. Thus the dilemma of "color" must ultimately be construed emblematically, with the ironic and unstated fact that human situations can *never* be as clear as "black and white."

In the antebellum South, much private security depended upon the public illusion that whites lived within a safe compound, that a barrier of insurmountable proportions separated them from the unknown horrors of some lesser existence, and that these territorial boundaries were clear and inviolable. The truth, of course, was that this was an uncertain margin, susceptible to a multitude of infractions and destined to prove unstable. At its very beginning, the story reminds us of inevitable change ahead: Désirée is presumed to have been left "by a party of Texans"—pioneers en route to the territory whose slave policies were so bitterly contested when it was annexed that they proved to be a significant precursor to the Civil War that followed. Chopin's touch is light: the implications of this detail may be lost to a modern audience, but they would have loomed mockingly to a reader in 1892, especially a Southern reader.

Even within the supposedly segregated social system there is abundant evidence of violation. "'And the way he cried,'" Désirée remarks proudly of her lusty child; "'Armand heard him the other day as far away as La Blanche's cabin.'" What color is La Blanche, we might wonder, and what was Armand's errand in her cabin? "One of La Blanche's little quadroon boys . . . stood fanning the child slowly," and he becomes a kind of nightmare double (perhaps a half-brother, in fact) for Désirée's baby—a visual clue to the secret of this infant's mixed blood; eventually, his presence provokes the shock of recognition for Désirée. "She looked from her child to the boy who stood beside him, and back again; over and over. 'Ah!' It was a cry that she could not help; which she was not conscious of having uttered." None of the "blacks" is referred to as actually dark-skinned; even the baby's caretaker is a "yellow nurse."

In the end, only Armand's skin is genuinely colored—a "dark, handsome face" momentarily brightened, it would seem, by the happiness of marriage. And if this description gives a literal clue to the denouement of the story's mystery, it is even more effective as an index to character. Armand has crossed that shadowy, demonic boundary between mercy and kindness on the one hand and cruelty on the other. His posture towards the slaves in his possession has always been questionable—his "rule was a strict one . . . and under it his negroes had forgotten how to be gay, as they had been during the old master's easygoing and indulgent lifetime." Little wonder, then, that when his wife's child displeases him, "the very spirit of Satan seemed suddenly to take hold of him." His inhumanity towards Désirée and the servants alike bespeaks an irreversible journey into some benighted region; and the bonfire, by whose light he reads that last, fateful letter, is no more than a visible sign of the triumph of those powers of darkness in his soul. Thus when Désirée exclaims wonderingly, "'my skin is fair. . . . Look at my hand; whiter than yours, Armand,'" her comment *may* be relevant to the parentage of each; however, within the context of the story, it figures more reliably as a guide to the boundaries of humane behavior.

Underlying this insistent preoccupation with the literal question of color, then, is Chopin's ironic perception of the tenuous quality of such distinctions: it is simplistic to call "quadroons" and "yellows" "blacks" and "negroes." And if we move from this overt level into the labyrinth of the human soul, we will discover a man who has become lost in the wilderness of his own "blackest" impulses—a master who reverts to tyranny and is possessed by Satan, by the only absolute darkness in the tale. The lesser existence into which Armand sinks stems not from his Negroid parentage, but from a potential for personal evil that he shares with all fellow creatures (as the leitmotif imagery of salvation and damnation suggests). Thus the horror that underlies Chopin's tale—and the ultimate mystery of "black and white" as she defines it—is not *really* limited to the social arrangements of the Southern slave system at all.

A world of evil is one sort of wilderness that lies along the margins of our most mundane activities, but it is not the only horror that lies in wait. Our moments of most joyful passion, too, threaten us with a form of annihilation: to be open to love is to be vulnerable to invasions that we can neither foresee nor fully protect ourselves against. Thus Chopin's rendering of the love between Désirée and Armand is an insistent compression of opposites. Armand is supposed to have fallen in love at first sight: "That was the way all the Aubignys fell in love, as if struck by a pistol shot. . . . The passion that awoke in him that day, when he saw her at the gate, swept along like an avalanche, or like a prairie fire, or like anything that drives headlong over all obstacles." The difference in Armand's life between love and some other force—something equally turbulent but more reckless and cruel—is no more than a hair's breadth or the fluttering of an eye. Linguistically, the two forces cannot be separated at all.

In Désirée's case, the peril of emotional entanglement has different origins; yet if anything, it is even more dangerous. She has been God's gift to her adoptive parents, the child of love as her name implies, helpless and delicate and unable to comprehend anything but love in its purest manifestations, "beautiful and gentle, affectionate and sincere,—the idol of Valmondé." Of the other side of love—of violence and baser passions—she is entirely innocent. In fact, innocence is her most marked characteristic, a kind of childlike, helpless ignorance. "It made [Madame Valmondé] laugh to think of Désirée with a baby. Why, it seemed but yesterday that Désirée was little more than a baby herself." Repeatedly, Chopin displays her infantine charm: Désirée couched with her baby, for example, "in her soft white muslins and laces," looking like nothing so much as a child herself. The vulnerability of such innocence is captured in her naive questions, in her trusting tendency to turn to her husband who has rejected her, even in the fragility of her garments that were surely intended only for one whose life might be protected from harsh contingencies. When Désirée married, she came to live at her husband's plantation, L'Abri (The Shelter); and such a home seems right, even necessary, for this delicate creature, even though the physical realities of the estate belie its name. "The roof came down steep and black like a cowl, reaching out beyond the wide galleries that encircled the yellow stuccoed house. Big, solemn oaks grew close to it, and thick-leaved, far-reaching branches shadowed it like a pall." However, Désirée must accept this refuge at mere face value: she cannot bring herself to see the ominous possibilities in those ancestral trees that portend both life and death.

In the end, Désirée cannot withstand the shock of being forced to acknowledge the contingencies whose existence she has ignored for so long. When Armand's love slips into cruelty, when L'Abri echoes with sibilant mockery, Désirée loses her own tenuous grasp on the balance of life. For her there seems only one choice, one final boundary to cross; and the alternatives are measured by the line between civilization and the patient, hungry bayou that lies just beyond. Madness, murder, death—all these wait to claim the love-child who could not keep her stability in the face of life's inescapable contrarieties. "She took the little one from the nurse's arms with no word of explanation, and descending the steps, walked away, under the live-oak branches. . . . Désirée had not changed the thin white garments nor the slippers which she wore. . . . She walked across a deserted field, where the stubble bruised her tender feet, so delicately shod, and tore her thin gown to shreds. She disappeared among the reeds and willows that grew thick along the banks of the deep, sluggish bayou; and she did not come back again."

Much of the effect of this tale derives from the understatement that Chopin employs to render Désirée's annihilation and Armand's inescapable, internal hell. Even more, perhaps, the effect comes from the economy with which she captures the precariousness of the human condition—the persistent shadow-line that threads its way through all of the significant transactions of our lives. This is, perhaps, the most consistent theme in all of Chopin's fictions. We can see it in her choice of subject—preoccupation with marriage that may be either destructive or replenishing, the relationship between mother and child that is both hindering of personal fulfillment and necessary for full womanly development, and the convulsive effects of emergent sexuality. We can see it even more subtly (but more insistently) in her imagistic patterns.

As early as the first novel Chopin was already focusing on the implications of that margin between the bayou and the transient clearing of the domesticated plantation, although her management of this theme is less skillful than it will become in later works. Mélicent is charmed by Grégoire's Southern passion and inclined to suppose that it is harmless—merely a game. Similarly, she is intrigued by the tropical bayou and disposed to project her simple, uncomplicated imagination into its dark recesses: "The wildness of the scene caught upon her erratic fancy, speeding it for a quick moment into the realms of romance." Very soon, Mélicent realizes that there is an unknowable, primitive force in the bayou's depth—something that both frightens and repels her. "Nameless voices—weird sounds that awake in a Southern forest at twilight's approach,—were crying a sinister welcome to the settling gloom." Eventually, she is shocked by a similarly ominous and irrational strain in Grégoire's passion for her, the hint of a potential for blind destruction. In both cases, Chopin demonstrates Mélicent's reluctance and innocence by showing her need to honor certain boundaries that society has drawn. She ventures out in the pirogue only once, shunning the bayou thereafter; eventually, she rejects the lover, too, by returning to the safety of her Northern home.

Much later, when she wrote *The Awakening*, Chopin would again employ this metaphor of margins (as she had throughout the many stories written between her first and second novels); and in this work the theme appears with consummate artistry. Here Chopin deals with the many implications of Edna Pontellier's emergent sexuality—both its positive and its destructive elements. The irresistible sensual call of the sun and sea echoes throughout the book to render the tidal pull of the heroine's nascent feelings; and throughout there is a linguistic insistence upon the significance of boundaries and of their violation. Indeed, the earliest descriptive passages announce the motif: we are at the beach where water meets land, sky meets water; and in the tropical white sun, demarcating lines waver uncertainly. "[Mr. Pontellier] fixed his gaze upon a white sunshade that was advancing at a snail's pace from the beach. He could see it plainly between the gaunt trunks of the water-oaks and across the stretch of yellow camomile. The gulf looked far away, melting hazily into the blue of the horizon." As the novel progresses, this initial statement of theme is expanded to include many paired possibilities—sleeping and waking, freedom and isolation, life and death—and the almost unendurable tension that is felt by all who must maintain a balanced separation between the warring opposites in life is suggested by Chopin's repeated use of the word "melting."

The vision in all of Chopin's best fiction is consummately interior, and it draws for strength upon her willingness to confront the bleak fact of life's tenuous stabilities. Read quite independently, "Désirée's Baby" may be judged a superb piece of short fiction—an economical, tight psychological drama. However, seen in the more ample context of Chopin's complete work, the story accrues added significance as the most vivid and direct statement of her major concern—the fiction of limits.

SUSAN J. ROSOWSKI

The Novel of Awakening

The bildungsroman or apprenticeship novel is defined by its theme. It is "a novel which recounts the youth and young manhood of a sensitive protagonist who is attempting to learn the nature of the world, discover its meaning and pattern, and acquire a philosophy of life and 'the art of living'" [C. Hugh Holman, *A Handbook to Literature,* Odyssey Press, 1972]. The definition and the examples that follow it are notably masculine, omitting developments of this theme in literature by and about women—the theme of awakening. The novel of awakening is similar to the apprenticeship novel in some ways: it also recounts the attempts of a sensitive protagonist to learn the nature of the world, discover its meaning and pattern, and acquire a philosophy of life, but she must learn these lessons in terms of herself as a woman. This difference results in other differences between the novel of awakening and the apprenticeship novel. The subject and action of the novel of awakening characteristically consist of a protagonist who attempts to find value in a world defined by love and marriage. The direction of awakening follows what is becoming a pattern in literature by and about women: movement is inward, toward greater self knowledge that leads in turn to a revelation of the disparity between that self knowledge and the nature of the world. The protagonist's growth results typically not with "an art of living," as for her male counterpart, but instead with a realization that for a woman such an art of living is difficult or impossible: it is an awakening to limitations. These elements of the novel of awakening may be illustrated by five representative

From *Genre* 12, no. 3 (Fall 1979). © 1979 by the University of Oklahoma.

novels: *Madame Bovary, The Awakening, My Mortal Enemy, Daughter of Earth,* and *Middlemarch.*

Flaubert's *Madame Bovary* is a prototype for the novel of awakening. Emma Bovary, a character who has learned the nature of the world through romantic fiction, struggles to acquire an art of living in accord with those fictional values. Conflict is largely internal, between two selves: an inner, imaginative self of private value is at odds with an outer, conventional self of social value. Movement is from an initial childhood separation between the two selves to an illusion of synthesis in marriage, followed by an awakening to the impossibility of such a union and a return to separation. Finally, like many other protagonists in the novel of awakening, Emma Bovary is essentially passive. Tension results from the reader's awareness of the impossibility—even undesirability—of her efforts: we ask what will happen to Emma Bovary, not what will she bring about, and we measure her greatness—her soul—by the extent to which she awakens to impossibilities.

In her childhood, Emma Rouault experienced a separation between two basic elements in herself—her private, imaginative self and her public, social self. Early she began to live a dual life: at school, the outward asceticism of a convent was at odds with inner excesses of religious mysticism and romantic dreams; at home, the realism and simplicity of farm life conflicted with dreams of luxury and bliss. Romantic fiction promises that separation between these two lives will end with marriage, when a girl will combine passionate love with public duties as a wife and mother. And so Emma Rouault, believing "qu'elle possédait enfin cette passion merveilleuse qui jusqu'alors s'était tenue comme un grand oiseau au plumage rose planant dans la splendeur des ciels poétiques," marries Charles Bovary.

Almost immediately disparity between dream and reality is evident, for Emma "ne pouvait s'imaginer à présent que ce calme où elle vivait fût le bonheur qu'elle avait rêvé." Tension builds as her imaginative self, shaped by romantic fantasies, finds no outlet in her role as a wife. By the time the Bovarys are invited to a ball given by a neighboring Marquis at la Vaubyessard, Emma has recognized that all her efforts to insert passionate love into her marriage have failed. Bored with her everyday existence, she perceives the ball as an incarnation of her earlier fantasy life, but with a difference. At the ball, imaginative value is maintained only by a complete separation from the human reality of time, and Emma ceases to perceive herself in terms of a past and a future: "sa vie passée, si nette jusqu'alors, s'évanouissait tout entière, et elle doutait presque de l'avoir vécue. Elle était là; puis autour du bal, il n'y avait plus que de l'ombre, étalée sur tout le reste."

It is against this fact of separation that Emma Bovary concentrates her resources. As a woman, however, her possibilities for action are limited: she believes her sex is dependent upon a man to initiate her "aux énergies de la passion, aux raffinements de la vie, à tous les mystères." No longer expecting to be satisfied by vicarious existence through her husband, Emma turns to other men—to a son and, finally, to lovers. While she is pregnant, "cette idée d'avoir pour enfant un mâle était comme la revanche en espoir de toutes ses impuissances passées. Un homme, au moins, est libre; il peut parcourir les passions et les pays, traverser les obstacles, mordre aux bonheurs les plus lointains. Mais une femme est empêchée continuellement. Inerte et flexible à la fois, elle a contre elle les mollesses de la chair avec les dépendances de la loi."

With the birth of a daughter, even this dream of vicarious extension is disproved, and Emma turns to imaginative value through lovers. Entering an affair with a neighboring landowner, Rodolphe Boulanger, Emma revels "à cette idée comme à celle d'une autre puberté qui lui serait survenue. . . . Elle entrait dans quelque chose de merveilleux où tout serait passion, extase, délire." More specifically, Emma again imagines release from the limitations of space and time: "une immensité bleuâtre l'entourait, les sommets du sentiment étincelaient sous sa pensée, et l'existence ordinaire n'apparaissait qu'an loin, tout en bas, dans l'ombre, entre les intervalles de ces hauteurs." Separation between her two lives remains complete: Emma imagines not joining her fantasy with everyday existence, but rather leaving everyday existence and entering a dream world of romantic love: "Elle devenait elle-même comme une partie veritable de ces imaginations et réalisait la longue rêverie de sa jeunesse, en se considérant dans ce type d'amoureuse qu'elle avait tant envié."

Tension in the novel of awakening results from the reader's awareness that the protagonist's attempts to escape human realities are impossible. Flaubert reminds us of this impossibility by counterposing characters that represent worldly concerns to Emma's dream of escape. Lheureux, a usurer, pursues Emma as a hunter pursues his victim, tightening his net about her as she becomes ensnared in debts taken on in desperate attempts to reproduce the luxurious life of her imagination; and the blind man symbolically pursues her, a stark reminder of the sickness, decay, and death that are inevitable elements of human existence.

Finally, then, change disproves Emma Bovary's dreams of romantic bliss. Her vision of a future with Rodolphe, "infini, harmonieux," ends when he abandons her. Her initial happiness with the clerk, Léon, ends when she rediscovers "dans l'adultère toutes les platitudes du mariage." Through change, Emma Bovary realizes the "impossibilitié" of her dream of everlasting bliss, for "tout plaisir [a] son dégoût, et les meilleurs baisers ne vous laissaient sur la lèvre qu'une irréalisable envie d'une volupté plus haute." Eventually, the tension between Emma's two lives becomes intolerable. Still seeking to satisfy the imaginative self formed in her childhood and wishing to escape "comme un oiseau, aller se rajeunir quelque part, bien loin, dans les espaces immaculés," Emma takes poison. In her last moments, the narrator comments, she undoubtedly rediscovers "au milieu d'un apaisement extraordinaire la volupté perdue de ses premiers élancements mystiques, avec des visions de béatitude éternelle qui commençaient."

But Emma Bovary's final vision is not rendered directly, for the perspective here is the narrator's. Indeed, throughout the novel, Flaubert maintains ironic distance from his protagonist: the reader more often observes than participates in Emma Bovary's awakening. In a later, American novel, *The Awakening*, Kate Chopin combines elements from *Madame Bovary* with a significant shift in focus. The ironic distance of *Madame Bovary* is replaced by a high degree of narrative sympathy. Written by a woman and focusing strictly upon changes of consciousness in its protagonist, *The Awakening* represents a distilled example of the novel of awakening.

The theme of limitation characteristic of the novel of awakening begins in the initial pages of *The Awakening*, in which the protagonist, Edna Pontellier, is presented as a passive embodiment of a social role. The omniscient narrator looks through Léonce Pontellier's eyes as he watches his wife approach, viewing her as he would "a valuable piece of personal property." But Edna Pontellier is stirred to dreams, and with her dreams comes the tension that will be developed through the rest of the novel. For like Emma Bovary, Edna has a "dual life—that outward existence which conforms, the inward life which questions." Her outward existence is that of social roles— the roles of wife and mother. Her inner life, on the other hand, is that of imaginative release through dreams. Through dreams, one may be freed from arbitrary measurements, as Edna was when she dreamed of walking across a big field in which she "'could see only the stretch of green before me, and I felt as if I must walk on forever, without coming to the end of it.'"

However, underlying this sense of imaginative freedom is a reality of limitation. When a child, Edna distinguished between the outer world of reality and the inner life of dreams; with her marriage, she had expected to end this duality by severing her connection with a dream life, for "as the devoted wife of a man who worshiped her, she felt she would take her place with a certain dignity in the world of reality, closing the portals forever behind her upon the realm of romance and dreams." As the novel progresses, the apparent calm of Edna's social role seen in the initial paragraphs is destroyed by her increasingly powerful responses to the sensuousness around her. With her emerging passions, Edna again becomes conscious of her own duality: her youthful romantic infatuations are transmuted into an adult combination of romance and sexuality. This revitalization climaxes when, while listening to piano music, Edna responds with her whole being: "the very passions themselves were aroused with her soul, swaying it, lashing it."

But, contrary to the illusion of independence offered by this revitalized inner self, Chopin describes the release of Edna's imaginative life in terms of passivity. Edna "blindly" follows "whatever impulse moved her, as if she had placed herself in alien hands for direction." At the heart of this passivity is Edna's attempt to escape from the objective world, for self-determination is impossible without taking into account the realities of human existence— time and change. Knowing the essential irreconcilability of her romantic dreams with reality, Edna carefully avoids any confrontation of the two. Her refrain that she will not think about the future runs like a motif throughout the novel. Attempting to protect her revitalized inner life, Edna physically and psychologically isolates herself, casting off family responsibilities, pursuing her solitary thoughts, and, finally, moving to her own house.

During this period, Edna's attempts to satisfy the need of her soul "for the unlimited in which to lose herself" take the classic feminine form of love. But her attempts to love are frustrated. Her emerging sexuality—the natural adult outgrowth of romantic longings—is developed by the rake, Arobin, in an alliance that leaves her dissatisfied, for it remains dissociated from love. Conversely, her love for the character most sympathetic in age and spirit to herself, Robert, leaves her dissatisfied also, for it remains dissociated from sex.

Finally, then, Edna, like Emma Bovary, completes the process of awakening by placing her romantic dreams for escape in the context of time and change. For the first time, she sees herself in terms of the past and the future: "she had said over and over to herself: 'To-day it is Arobin; to-morrow it will be some one else.'" Edna's suicide represents her final attempt to escape—to escape her children, her lovers, and, most important, time and change. For only by complete isolation of self can Edna be truthful to her inner life. Any contact with external reality threatens this dream. Thus Edna, while swimming to sea and death, returns to her childhood dreams of limitlessness, recalling the meadow of her youth and her belief that "it had no beginning and no end."

Imagery describing Edna Pontellier's death is similar to that describing Emma Bovary's death. Both characters, experiencing the expanding consciousness basic to the growth of the child into an adult, come to the age-

old realization of the conflict between the soul's yearning for the infinite
pitted against the body's imprisonment in the finite. But the protagonist for
this realization is traditionally male: he must learn to concentrate his energies
in work that, by having broad social and ethical implications, will transcend
his own mortality. Flaubert and Chopin, using women as their protagonists,
add to thematic tension by including sexist roles which restrict the woman
from the expansion necessary to deal with her realization. Alternatives are
severely limited to feminine ones: the woman must choose between her inner
life of romance and the outer world of reality. Either alternative leaves her
passive: when she is true to her romantic dreams, she is the passive pawn of
her own moods; when she attempts to follow the outer world, she is the
passive pawn of men—of a husband or a lover. More important, the dreams
in which she attempts to lose herself are limited: she regresses to childhood
dreams of limitlessness or she loses herself in romantic dreams of passion.

In her 1899 review of *The Awakening*, Willa Cather comments on
Flaubert's and Chopin's limiting their characters' inner lives to the traditionally feminine mode of romantic love. Cather writes,

> Edna Pontellier and Emma Bovary are studies in the same femi-
> nine type. . . . Both women belong to a class, not large, but for-
> ever clamoring in our ears, that demands more romance out of
> life than God put into it. . . . they are the victims of the over-
> idealization of love. . . . These people really expect the passion of
> love to fill and gratify every need of life, whereas nature only
> intended that it should meet one of many demands. They insist
> upon making it stand for all the emotional pleasures of life and
> art; expecting an individual and self-limited passion to yield in-
> finite variety, pleasure, and distraction, and to contribute to their
> lives what the arts and the pleasurable exercise of the intellect
> gives to less limited and less intense idealists. So this passion,
> when set up against Shakespeare, Balzac, Wagner, Raphael, fails
> them. They have staked everything on one hand, and they lose.
> They have driven the blood until it will drive no further, they
> have played their nerves up to the point where any relaxation
> short of absolute annihilation is impossible. . . . And in the end,
> the nerves get even. Nobody ever cheats them, really. Then the
> "awakening" comes.

Later, in *My Mortal Enemy*, Cather presents her own version of an
awakening, concentrating upon the moral implications to women of this
feminine type who are "the victims of the over-idealization of love." The

awakening in *My Mortal Enemy* develops in an almost symmetrically inverse direction from that of *Madame Bovary* and *The Awakening*. Emma Bovary and Edna Pontellier move from reality to dream; Myra Henshawe moves from dream to reality.

This movement occurs in three stages, corresponding to the meetings between the narrator, Nellie Birdseye, and Myra Henshawe. In the first stage, the dream is dominant as Nellie recounts the story of the elopement of Myra Driscoll and Oswald Henshawe. For this story, Cather draws heavily upon a stock romantic situation. Myra Driscoll is the one-dimensional romantic heroine, "an orphan" who "had been brought up by her great-uncle" in a manner worthy of a fairy tale: she "had everything: dresses and jewels, a fine riding horse, a Steinway piano." The romantic pattern continues with her falling in love with the dashing Oswald Henshawe. The young lovers meet the opposition of their elders, the result of "an old grudge of some kind," and, although Myra's uncle threatens disinheritance, they secretly elope. In presenting this story, Cather foreshadows her thematic concern with the moral implications of the romantic myth. The story of Myra and Oswald's elopement becomes an enticing social convention for, as Nellie recalls, Myra "and her runaway marriage were the theme of the most interesting, indeed the only interesting, stories that were told in our family on holidays or at family dinners."

The serious thematic question about this process is identified by Nellie, who initiates the theme of awakening to be developed in the rest of the novel. Refusing to allow the romantic tale to remain in the distant past, she asks about the consequences of the lovers' actions: despite the fact that they were disinherited, have the lovers " 'been happy, anyhow' "? The rather off-hand reply to her question, " 'Happy? Oh, yes! As happy as most people,' " elicits Nellie's reflection, "That answer was disheartening; the very point of their story was that they should be much happier than other people." The question implicit in this response is similar to the objection Cather raises to Flaubert's and Chopin's protagonists: what is the "point" of the romantic legend that idealizes love?

In developing a response to the question, Cather makes two basic modifications in focus from *Madame Bovary* and *The Awakening*: the earlier two novels presented protagonists married to men obviously unsuited to them in both age and temperament. Only the thinnest illusion of love ever existed within marriage: they awaken to both the power and the limitation of romantic love outside of marriage. Cather, however, places romantic love within marriage. And the earlier two novels present a relatively specific time in the lives of their protagonists: neither Emma Bovary nor Edna Pontellier lives to the full maturity of old age. Cather, however, gives temporal change a major role by taking Myra Driscoll Henshawe from childhood to old age. Indeed, the dominant reality within which the awakening of *My Mortal Enemy* occurs is the human reality of change.

In the opening scenes of *My Mortal Enemy,* the incongruity between the figures in the legend and the characters themselves stress temporal change: the Myra Driscoll Henshawe of the romantic legend, an ageless heroine, is rather grotesquely unlike "the real Myra Henshawe," who, at "forty-five," is "a short, plump woman in a black velvet dress." Similarly, though not quite so obviously, in the initial pages Cather introduces change through Nellie Birdseye, for the naive young girl who had been told the romantic tale of Myra Henshawe "ever since [she] could remember anything at all" is strikingly different from the complex narrator, recounting her childhood memories with the human compassion possible only with adult understanding. The child Nellie represents the romantic perspective of escape from time: she thinks of the Driscoll place, for example, "as being under a spell, like the Sleeping Beauty's palace; it had been in a trance, or lain in its flowers like a beautiful corpse, ever since that winter night when Love went out of the gates and gave the dare to Fate"; the narrator Nellie provides a counterpoint of reality by recalling, "I knew that this was not literally true."

This underlying discrepancy between romance and reality is defined sharply at the time of the second meeting between Myra and Nellie, now in New York. Here the emphasis is upon the disparity between the romantic legend and human reality: Myra emerges from the myth to become a complex character, directly questioning the morality of advancing others in love. She reflects to Nellie, "'See the moon coming out, Nellie—behind the tower. It wakens the guilt in me. No playing with love; and I'd sworn a great oath never to meddle again. You send a handsome fellow . . . to a fine girl . . . and it's Christmas eve, and they rise above us, and the white world around us, and there isn't anybody, not a tramp on the park benches, that wouldn't wish them well—and very likely hell will come of it!'" This emphasis on moral consequences of human action is raised also by development in the character of Nellie. Nellie has passed into adolescence, the stage of her own life at which young women conventionally commit themselves to a romantic concept of love and marriage. For Nellie, the Henshawes represent such a concept: she is, when she visits them, "'fair moon-struck.'"

But again, contrast with human realities belies the myth. Throughout this section, Nellie stresses complexities. Myra's generosity with her friends is contrasted with her bitterness at her poverty. The apparent happiness of the Henshawes is contrasted with their intrigue and deceit in seemingly trivial matters. Most important, Nellie's romanticism is contrasted to her growing sensitivity to the human complexity of Myra Henshawe. Seeing Myra's unhappiness over her poverty, Nellie "glimpsed what seemed to me insane ambition," a judgment that is countered in the next scene by Nellie's appreciation of Myra's brilliance and charm with her friends: "Their talk quite took my breath away; they said such exciting, such fantastic things about people, books, music—anything; they seemed to speak together a kind of highly flavored special language." Finally, Nellie realizes that Myra's "chief extravagance was in caring for so many people and in caring for them so much."

At the end of this section, separations result from widening disparities between romantic expectations and human realities; and the transmission of the romantic myth from one generation to another is interrupted. The realities of their own lives force Myra and Oswald into petty, jealous quarrels and, eventually, into a temporary separation. Witnessing this quarrel, Nellie awakens to the human complexity in a marriage and, her romantic sensibility deeply disillusioned by her perception, she leaves the Henshawes to move into the adult phase of her own life.

At the time of their third meeting, ten years later, realism is dominant, inescapably revealed in both setting and action. The setting is "a sprawling overgrown Westcoast city which was in the throes of rapid development—it ran about the shore, stumbling all over itself and finally tumbled untidily into the sea." Here Nellie Birdseye finds the Henshawes, living in a "shabby, comfortless place." Physical changes extend to the Henshawes themselves: Oswald has "thin white hair and stooped shoulders" and "the tired, tired face of one who has utterly lost hope." But no such simple description could portray Myra Henshawe. In this last, most developed section, Myra Henshawe completely belies the simplistic, one-dimensional character of the romantic myth: when Nellie finds her, "she sat crippled but powerful in her brilliant wrappings. She looked strong and broken, generous and tyrannical, a witty and rather wicked old woman, who hated life for its defeats and loved it for its absurdities." Most important, Myra has awakened to the personal consequences of her romantic elopement with Oswald: " 'It's been the ruin of us both. We've destroyed each other.' "

In developing this realization of Myra's, Cather incorporates into *My Mortal Enemy* her objection to Flaubert and Chopin's protagonists: the Henshawes' elopement and marriage represent an attempt to live according to the romantic myth that "the passion of love [may] fill and gratify every need of life, whereas nature only intended that it should meet one of many demands." As Myra explains to Nellie, " 'People can be lovers and enemies at the same time, you know. We were. . . . A man and a woman draw apart from that long embrace, and see what they have done to each other. Perhaps I can't forgive him for the harm I did him. Perhaps that's it. When there are children, that feeling goes through natural changes. But when it remains so personal . . . something gives way in one.' " It is the "individual and self-limited" nature of romantic passion that is destructive, for by definition such passion restricts one from expansive movement toward great truths. As in her review of *The Awakening,* in *My Mortal Enemy* Cather contrasts this limited passion to the greater variety of passion provided by the arts: she develops in Myra a potential for greatness, portraying her soul's yearnings for the universal values represented by music and literature. Thus, at the end of her life, Myra seeks the solace of constants: she returns to religion, nature, and literature.

With her description of Myra Henshawe's death, Cather presents an expansive movement toward metaphysical truths that reverse the commitment to an inner life of dreams seen in Emma Bovary and Edna Pontellier. Myra Henshawe realizes her soul's need for universal values, and she acts in accord with this realization. Nellie recognizes in Myra's dying actions "a yearning strong enough to lift that ailing body and drag it out into the world again." Removing herself from the shabby hotel room which represents the consequences of her early commitment to romantic passion, Myra uses one of her gold pieces to hire a cab to go to the cliff that reminds her of Lear. There she meets death with religion and art. Later, Nellie finds "her wrapped in her blankets, leaning against the cedar trunk, facing the sea. Her head had fallen forward; the ebony crucifix was in her hands. She must have died peacefully and painlessly. There was every reason to believe she had lived to see the dawn."

In the final pages, Cather continues the outward movement of her theme of awakening through Nellie Birdseye. Throughout the novel, the relation between Myra and Nellie has been that of tutor to student: the older woman initially represents to Nellie the traditional romantic myth. By the time of their second meeting, Myra emerges from the dream to act as a human tutor to Nellie. In the last pages, Myra's cry, " 'if youth but knew!' " calls for an extension of the theme of awakening into the future. This final movement begins with Myra, who utters the words from which the title is taken, " 'Why must I die like this, alone with my mortal enemy?' " Nellie responds with "dread," for she "had never heard a human voice utter such a terrible judgment upon all one hopes for." But, as she must in her growth toward personal identity, Nellie completes the process alone. After her initial revulsion, Nellie grew calmer and "began to understand a little what she meant." And later, after the death of Myra Henshawe, Nellie continues her own awakening. In these final pages, Nellie does not reject love itself, nor does she experience a "disillusionment [that] leaves her hopeless." Throughout the novel, Nellie is markedly different from Myra Henshawe, for, as Nellie points out, she has youth, and "for youth there is always the hope, the certainty, of better things." What Nellie *does* reject is the over idealization of love that occurs when "*a common feeling* [is] exalted into beauty by imagination, generosity, and the flaming courage of youth" (my emphasis). With this understanding, Nellie has the potential to move into the future without the self-limiting romantic illusion of the young Myra Driscoll Henshawe or of Chopin's Edna Pontellier: she has the potential to become the narrator of *My Mortal Enemy,* with the capacity to understand and appreciate the complexly human woman, Myra. It is, then, Nellie who completes the theme of the novel in her awakening to the limitations of the romantic myth—a myth that insists people fit themselves into simplistic categories that ignore the complexities of time and change. By the end of *My Mortal Enemy,* the character Nellie joins the narrator Nellie. The strength of the book lies in the growth that has resulted in this union, making possible the narrator's tone as she combines compassion and objectivity to tell of Myra Driscoll Henshawe's human complexities, her combination of meanness and greatness, worldliness and spirituality, hatred and love.

Myra Driscoll Henshawe awakened to limitations accompanying romantic love and to the freedom offered by metaphysical truths; her awakening remained, however, within the confines of a marriage based on romantic love. Only through the narrator, Nellie Birdseye, is there the possibility of growth beyond such confines. With Marie Rogers, the protagonist of Agnes Smedley's *Daughter of Earth,* the awakening to limitations ensuing from conventions of romantic love occurs as an early step in a larger process. In one sense, then, *Daughter of Earth* begins where *My Mortal Enemy* leaves off, with a turning away from romantic love and toward commitment to a higher value. The adult narrator, Marie Rogers, introduces the narrative with such a commitment: "Now I stand at the end of one life and on the threshold of another. Contemplating. Weighing. About me lie the ruins of a life. Instead of blind faith,—directness, unbounded energy; and instead of unclearness, I now have the knowledge that comes from experience; work that is limitless in its scope and significance. Is not this enough to weigh against love?" The rest of the novel retraces Marie Rogers's development to that point of commitment, beginning with "the first thing I remember of life."

A major difference between Marie Rogers and previous protagonists of novels of awakening—Emma Bovary, Edna Pontellier, and Myra Driscoll

Henshawe—lies in their childhoods. Unlike the luxury in which Emma,
Edna, and Myra were raised—luxury that provided time and materials for
romantic fantasies—the deprivation of Marie Rogers's youth meant "there
was but one thing on which I could depend—poverty and uncertainty." And
unlike protagonists to whom female models of passivity and subservience
promised happiness, to Marie such models led only to poverty and misery.
Marie's mother married for love; at thirty, she was a woman worn old by
endless work and disappointment. In Marie's childhood, the girls or women
granted the most respect were those who followed male patterns, Marie's
Aunt Mary, "a woman with the body and mind of a man," and her aunt
Helen, who demonstrated that "to be a hired girl drawing your own money
gave you a position of authority and influence in the community."

Thus for the girl Marie, the reality of everyday existence belied any
romantic fiction of happiness through love. She came to believe that "the
true position of the husband and wife in the marriage relationship" was that
marriage made women subservient and men tyrannical. More basically, the
"little drama of the lowly" in which Marie participated disproved the fun-
damental dream of happiness for the just: "On the one hand stretched my
world of fairy tales, the song of 'The Maple Leaves Forever,' the tales of good
little girls being kind to animals, of color, dancing, music, with happiness in
the end even if things were not all right now. On the other hand stood—a
little house with a rag pasted over a broken window-pane; a lone struggling
morning-glory trying to live in the baked soil before the porch; Annie being
dragged by her tousled streaming hair; my father, once so straight and handsome, now a round-shouldered man with tobacco juice showing at the cor-
ners of his mouth."

Initially, limitations imposed on the child Marie created both an intellectual and an emotional blindness. Intellectually, she knew nothing of the
world outside the narrow confines of an illiterate family on the lowest eco-
nomic rung of society; emotionally, she learned that "love and tenderness
meant only pain and suffering and defeat." To survive, she suppressed all
such emotions: "I was a savage beast and I harbored injuries and hatreds in
my heart. Right or wrong, it is true. It is. The ways of life had taught me
no tenderness."

From this early blindness, the process of awakening moves in two directions. First, commitment to outward, intellectual expansion through education and work provides the basic structure of the novel: Marie goes from
a child of poverty to a grade school student, to kitchen help, to teacher in
New Mexico, to travelling magazine saleswoman, to student in Arizona and
California, to journalist in New York and, finally, to dedicated socialist and

revolutionary of the Indian Movement. Redefinition of values accompanies this outward physical progression. Marie's goals were initially conventional and materialistic: beginning her higher education, for example, she felt "before me now lay a university degree; and beyond—well, it might be position, one day money and power." Gradually, however, Marie turns from this early materialism until, through study with a teacher in the Indian Movement, she "touched for the first time a movement of unwavering principle and beauty—the struggle of a continent to be free." The result represents the climax of Marie's growth toward intellectual awakening; she achieves identity and value and, with them, a basis for action: "The Indian work was the first thing I had ever suffered for out of principle, from choice. It was not just living, just reacting to life—it was expression. It gave me a sense of self-respect, of dignity, that nothing else had ever given me."

Simultaneously, the second direction of awakening develops Marie's emotional self. Her capacity for tenderness grows in her increasing affection for her mother, her friends, and, finally, in her ability to love a man. But as the two selves in Marie develop, tension results from their contradictory demands. Marie has learned from experience that the needs for work and for love are not only incompatible but, for a woman, mutually destructive. As Marie matures, she resists any affection she feels for members of her family, resolving "I would not let [love] ruin me as it ruined others!" Similarly, Marie resists affection toward men and the accompanying integration of sex with love: for her, "sex had no place in love. Sex meant violence, marriage or prostitution, and marriage meant children, weeping nagging women and complaining men; it meant unhappiness, and all the things that I feared and dreaded and intended to avoid." Unable to resolve the "war being waged within my own spirit, a war between my need and desire of love, and the perverted idea of love and sex that had ground into my being from my first breath," Marie separates from her first husband.

This increasing tension between the needs for work and for love comes to a climax when Marie falls in love with and marries Anand, a fellow worker in the Indian Movement. In this relationship she, like other women in novels of awakening, attempts to unify the private and public lives she had previously kept separate. Gradually, however, jealousy and misunderstanding occur both between Marie and Anand and among other workers in the Indian Movement, and eventually the relationship threatens their work. Recognizing that "our love . . . was destroying us," they separate, and the book returns to its beginning, with the sacrifice of love for freedom.

The awakening of Marie Rogers is, like other awakenings of women in literature, an awakening to limitation and conflict—to the inevitable conflict between the need for personal love and the need for meaningful public action. And, like other protagonists of novels of awakening, Marie sacrifices love for freedom. But the nature of that sacrifice differs radically from that of Emma Bovary or Edna Pontellier, for Marie Rogers defines freedom in terms of worldly action and work that are liberating in their broad social and ethical implications. In this sense, she is similar to male protagonists of the bildungsroman.

Behind this affirmation of freedom in work are certain other characteristics that distinguish Marie Rogers. First, she does not seek to escape time. The major awakening in *Daughter of Earth*—that to the Indian Movement— is valuable precisely because Marie is so intensely aware that the basic human realities are of change and death, for "life itself is the one glorious, eternal experience, and . . . there is no place here on this spinning ball of earth and stone for anything but freedom. For we reach scarce a hundred before we take our place by the side of those whom we have directly or indirectly injured, enslaved, or killed." For Marie, only the conviction of ideas releases one from temporal limitations. Imprisoned in The Tombs, she contrasts herself with other women prisoners: "They were physical women—as I had once been physical. But now I had some measure of thought, some measure of belief in the power of ideas; in this only did I differ from them. When the world, with its eating and sleeping, its dancing and singing, its colors and laughter, was taken from these women, they were without understanding or resistance. It was easy to make beasts of such women. They had nothing to support themselves with."

Second, Marie Rogers differs from the earlier protagonists of the novel by the extent to which she takes responsibility for herself: she quite simply refuses to accept the passivity and dependency so characteristic of the thinking of Emma Bovary and Edna Pontellier. And third, Marie moves outward to a far broader context than is evident in most novels of awakening: her expanding consciousness is measured by awareness of such figures as Emma Goldman and of such events as women's sufferage, miners' efforts to unionize, the IWW, WWI, and, most importantly, the Indian freedom movement.

Emma Bovary and Marie Rogers represent the extremes in the novel of awakening, the one imprisoned within an imagination shaped by romantic myths and the other committed to a movement for freedom on the other side of the globe. Most novels of awakening fall between the extremes, as represented by George Eliot's *Middlemarch*. In Dorothea Brooke, George Eliot presents a female character of great soul, searching for "something beyond the shallows of ladies'-school literature." The novel begins with Dorothea's sense of disparity between her needs as a human being and the role expected of her as a woman: "What could she do, what ought she to do?—she, hardly more than a budding woman, but yet with an active conscience and a great mental need, not to be satisfied by a girlish instruction comparable to the nibblings and judgments of a discursive mouse."

The pattern is similar to that of other novels of awakening: a young girl, denied direct experience of life, shapes her imaginative existence through literature and views marriage as the means by which the inner life of the imagination will join with the world of action. In the opening pages, romantic illusion characterizes Dorothea, who, "with all her eagerness to know the truths of life, retained very childlike ideas about marriage. She felt sure that she would have accepted the judicious Hooker, if she had been born in time to have him from that wretched mistake he made in matrimony; or John Milton when his blindness had come on." Dorothea's romantic hero takes a different form from that of Emma Bovary or Edna Pontellier; the blindness is similar, however, as are the results. Seeking deliverance "from her girlish subjection to her own ignorance," Dorothea marries Edward Casaubon, an elderly scholar whom Dorothea has transformed imaginatively into "a living Bosseut . . . a modern Augustine who united the glories of doctor and saint."

Two major stages occur in Dorothea's awakening. In the first, Dorothea recognizes and comes to terms with the results of her own blindness. On their wedding trip, both Dorothea and Edward Casaubon experience the disparity between their illusions about marriage and its reality. For Dorothea, this experience initially involves the vague feeling "that the large vistas and wide fresh air which she had dreamed of finding in her husband's mind were replaced by anterooms and winding passages which seemed to lead no-whither." Finally, following a disagreement, she begins "to see that she had been under a wild illusion in expecting a response to her feeling from Mr. Casaubon, and she had felt the waking of a presentiment that there might be a sad consciousness in his life which made as great a need on his side as on her own." Her awakening sympathy is crucial, for with it comes outward movement, to realistic perception of the world and her place in it, and to a moral response to this world. Dorothea thus turns from "the moral stupidity [of] taking the world as an udder to feed our supreme selves" to the enlarged and, finally, liberating awareness that others have "an equivalent centre of self, whence the lights and shadows must always fall with a certain difference."

Growth occurs from this point. In her relation to Casaubon, Dorothea struggles for "resolved submission." In the process, she passes from her dream of herself as "a lamp-holder" assisting "the highest purposes of truth" to duty as a "new form of inspiration" giving "a new meaning to wifely love." Here Dorothea's search for what she could do and what she ought to do takes a typically feminine form: Dorothea is an exceptional person, fully conscious that her husband's needs necessitate her denial of all that is most vital in herself; and she experiences a "benumbing" helplessness at the situation. But she is simultaneously committed to her sense of a moral ideal—her greatness lies, in fact, in this commitment. Dorothea's sense of "only the ideal and not the real yoke of marriage" leads to her submission to Casaubon while he is alive and, finally, to his anticipated request that after his death she dedicate herself to his work.

The second stage of awakening—to personal growth in love—occurs not with Casaubon's death but with the terms of his will revoking Dorothea's inheritance if she marries his nephew, Will Ladislaw. The result for Dorothea is personal rebirth. Upon hearing of the will, she has a "vague, alarmed consciousness that her life was taking on a new form, that she was undergoing a metamorphosis in which memory would not adjust itself to the stirring of new organs." Dorothea's metamorphosis involves release from her illusion that her marriage with Casaubon was like an ideal relationship: she experiences "a violent shock of repulsion from her departed husband, who had had hidden thoughts, perhaps perverting everything she said and did." Simultaneously, she "was conscious of another change which also made her tremulous: it was a sudden strange yearning of heart towards Will Ladislaw" and an opening to the possibility of love between them.

From this second major awakening, movement toward the union of Dorothea and Will Ladislaw follows: Dorothea experiences "the first sense of loving and being loved"; their relationship is thwarted by Dorothea's misunderstanding of Ladislaw's actions toward the married Rosamond Vincy and ends finally with understanding, shared commitment, and marriage. This second major phase of awakening is based, as the first was, on Dorothea's yearning "towards the perfect Right, that it might make a throne within her, and rule her errant will" and her feeling "the largeness of the world" and that "she was part of that involuntary, palpitating life, and could neither look out on it from her luxurious shelter as a mere spectator, nor hide her eyes in selfish complaining." But Dorothea's adjustment to this large moral sense is basically one of personal will and perspective: her attempts to act, whether to plan better housing for tenants or to assist the idealistic young physician, Lydgate, remain severely restricted by her position as a woman.

In this outcome, Dorothea Brooke is representative of women in other novels of awakening—Elizabeth Bennet, Emma Woodhouse, Isabel Archer—who are capable of dual movement, both inward to self knowledge and outward, toward awareness of social, ethical, and philosophical truths, but whose awakenings are to limitations and whose achievements are measured by their adjustments to their role as women. Many, like Dorothea, find extension to the world through marriage to a man whom they both respect and love. In the final chapter of *Middlemarch*, for example, Eliot describes the marriage of Dorothea and Will Ladislaw, a union bound by strong love in which "Will become an ardent public man," working for the reforms Dorothea had yearned for in her youth, and Dorothea gave him "wifely help." But few authors comment so directly as George Eliot on this special role of the exceptional woman in a world shaped by men: "Many who knew [Dorothea], thought it a pity that so substantive and rare a creature should have been absorbed into the life of another, and be only known in a certain circle as a wife and mother. But no one stated exactly what else that was in her power she ought rather to have done."

Thus, in their quite different approaches to their common subject, these five novels provide a starting place for discussion of the novel of awakening. All present protagonists who seek value in a world which expects a woman to define herself by love, marriage, and motherhood. For each, an inner, imaginative sense of personal value conflicts with her public role: an awakening occurs when she confronts the disparity between her two lives. As is illustrated by these five novels, treatments of this common theme differ dramatically. For Emma Bovary and Edna Pontellier, the primary movement of awakening is inward, to private imaginative values; for Myra Driscoll Henshawe and Marie Rogers, primary movement is outward, to metaphysical, moral, and social values. Dorothea Brooke's initial awakening of a moral sense prepares for a second awakening of love. But after noting these differences, we return to similarities among the novels. Each presents an awakening to limitations. Each presents a resolution only at great cost to the protagonist: she must deny one element of herself, whether by the extreme of Emma's and Edna's suicides or by Dorothea's turning from a direct, active public life. And, finally, each presents the dilemma of the individual who attempts to find value in a society that relegates to her only roles and values of the woman, ignoring her needs as a human being.

JOYCE C. DYER

Gouvernail, Kate Chopin's Sensitive Bachelor

Readers who know Chopin's short fiction before 1899 will recognize familiar faces and names in *The Awakening*. Madame Lebrun, Tonie Bocaze, Madame Antoine, Claire Duvigné, and Gouvernail all appear in Chopin works written prior to her end-of-the-century masterpiece. The reappearance of such characters gives Chopin's southern Louisianan community continuity and credibility. The stories maintain artistic autonomy and yet appear strangely related to one another. And, because we have met these characters before, we frequently see more in what they do and say during the course of the novel than we might otherwise.

For example, we remember "At Chênière Caminada" immediately and vividly when we encounter Chopin's comment in *The Awakening* about Tonie Bocaze, a Chênière Caminada fisherman and sailor: "He was shy, and would not willingly face any woman except his mother." We can hardly keep from smiling. In her 1893 story, Chopin had given us rather specific information about Tonie's "timidity." Underneath his shyness we were shown "the savage instinct of his blood" at work. Claire Duvigné (like Edna and Robert) had hired Tonie and his boat with the red lateen-sail. While out on the sea with her, he engaged in wild sexual fantasies; after their return to shore, "He was stirred by a terrible, an overmastering regret, that he had not clasped [Claire] in his arms when they were out there alone, and sprung with her into the sea."

From *Southern Literary Journal* 14, no. 1 (Fall 1981). © 1981 by the Department of English of the University of North Carolina at Chapel Hill.

However, it is Gouvernail whose past history and characterization become truly significant to the thematic, emotional, and imaginative experience
of Chopin's second novel. Gouvernail's appearance in *The Awakening* is
brief: he is merely one of nine guests who have been invited to Edna's twenty-
ninth birthday party in chapter 30. But the reader who knows Gouvernail
from "A Respectable Woman" (1894) and "Athénaise" (1895) quickly recognizes the full importance of his attendance at Edna's birthday celebration.
Gouvernail's previous understanding of sex, women, and passion, as well as
his earlier display of a poetic and deeply profound reticence adds to the
significance of his presence at Edna's round mahogany table.

In "A Respectable Woman," Mr. Baroda invites Gouvernail, his former
friend from college, to spend several days on the Barodas' plantation. Mrs.
Baroda, who rather resents her husband's asking the journalist to visit since
she had been looking forward to "undisturbed tête-à-tête" with her husband,
forms a mental image of the stranger. She imagines him the socially awkward
intellectual whose eccentric reading habits and poor attention to physical
well-being have left him with dim vision and a meager form: "She pictured
him, tall, slim, cynical; with eyeglasses, and his hands in his pockets." But
after he arrives, she discovers how false her preconceptions have been. Gouvernail is neither very tall nor irritatingly cynical. His manner toward the
Barodas is gracious and courteous. He immediately treats Mrs. Baroda with
inborn respect. Unlike many men, Gouvernail, polite and gentle always,
makes no conscious attempt to seek Mrs. Baroda's approval or in any way
to impress her.

Gouvernail and his unusual manner soon alarm Mrs. Baroda; he is not
what she has expected. Perhaps in some vague way the unpredictability of
Gouvernail's nature presents to Mrs. Baroda the possibility that her own
behavior may not be fully predictable. She has anticipated a man of ideas,
an intellectual somewhat out of touch with common matters and, even, simple sensations. Rather, Gouvernail proves to be a man excited by natural
pleasure perhaps even more than by "Ideas." He has already arrived at his
philosophy; it consists of an "acquiescence to the existing order—only a
desire to be permitted to exist, with now and then a little whiff of genuine
life." And "genuine life" for Gouvernail often means sensuous experience.
"This is what I call living," utters Gouvernail as the air sweeping across
Gaston Baroda's sugar field caresses him "with its warm and scented velvety
touch." The journalist even experiences pleasure from having the Barodas'
enormous dogs rub against his legs. And Gouvernail, suitably, exhibits little
desire to disrupt the natural world that brings him so much satisfaction:

going fishing or accompanying Gaston into the woods to kill grosbecs are activities he deliberately shuns.

On the night that Mrs. Baroda is unexpectedly joined by Gouvernail as she sits on a bench near a gravel walk, Gouvernail recites lines from section 21 of Whitman's *Song of Myself* to help him describe the sensuous pleasure the darkness affords. "'Night of south winds—night of the large few stars! / Still nodding night—,'" he murmurs, half to himself. The apostrophe, as Lewis Leary notes, becomes increasingly interesting after the reader supplies the phrases that precede and follow those chosen by Gouvernail: "Press close bare-bosm'd night"; "mad naked summer night." Leary suggests that Chopin's technique of omission here was quite conscious: she obviously knew the lines that came before those she quoted, and she probably hoped her readers would recognize nuances "which in the 1890s [Chopin] might not openly express."

But an interesting question still remains. Might we assume that the omission allows us to make certain inferences about the speaker who makes it as well as about the author herself? Bernard Koloski thinks so. He feels the lines indicate that Gouvernail "is sensitive to the sexual longings which are at the moment shaking his friend's wife." His observation seems supportable and, even, capable of some expansion. Chopin's careful artistry throughout this story permits us to at least consider that Gouvernail himself, consciously or half-consciously, is telling us (and certainly Mrs. Baroda) more about the "little whiff of genuine life" he is experiencing on this occasion than he dare with words so soon in their acquaintance. Gouvernail, like Mrs. Baroda, might also be experiencing the turbulence of passion. Perhaps it is not only the still, warm night and baneful air that arouse him. Certainly the omitted lines suggest that Mrs. Baroda's sexuality is in part responsible for his enjoyment of the night and for his desire to speak "intimately [to Mrs. Baroda] in a low, hesitating drawl that was not unpleasant to hear." And we cannot help but think that Gouvernail's gesture of offering Mrs. Baroda a white, filmy scarf to cover herself (a shawl, incidentally, that she lets lie in her lap) symbolizes the same kind of temporary veiling of passion and sex that we later see by his crucial Whitman omission. At the very least, then, Gouvernail's motive for selecting the lines he does is ironically ambiguous. At the very most, his motive is passion tempered by a natural respect for women, a sensitivity to Mrs. Baroda's position, and patient self-control.

Mrs. Baroda certainly senses the sexual mood of the night—if not the mood of Gouvernail himself. Her physical being predominates. As she drinks in the tones of her visitor's low voice, she wants "to reach out her hand in the darkness and touch him with the sensitive tips of her fingers upon the face or lips," "to draw close to him and whisper against his cheek—she did not care what—as she might have done if she had not been a respectable woman." Earlier, Chopin assured us that the apostrophe to the night "indeed, was not addressed to [Mrs. Baroda]." However, Chopin's narrative statement may have been more than a little ironic; Mrs. Baroda responds as if Whitman's lines were meant for her, and Gouvernail selects them, perhaps, with some knowledge of their sexual implications for the situation at hand.

In "Athénaise," Gouvernail befriends the lovely daughter of the Michés during her separation from her husband, Cazeau. In this story, Gouvernail's personality and values become far more precisely defined than they are in "A Respectable Woman." Chopin lets us know what he is thinking as he accompanies Athénaise about the New Orleans streets and talks with her in the Dauphine Street apartment house where both he and she rent rooms from Sylvie. We learn about Gouvernail in several of the story's eleven sections. His intelligence, his respectful manner, his sensuality, his maturity— even his physical appearance find elaboration in the tale of Athénaise.

Before meeting Gouvernail, Athénaise, like Mrs. Baroda, had pictured him falsely in her mind. Sylvie had only told her of his luxurious furnishings and many volumes of books. Athénaise imagined him "a stout, middle-aged gentleman, with a bushy beard turning gray, wearing large gold-rimmed spectacles, and stooping somewhat from much bending over books and writing materials." But as it turns out, Gouvernail is rather attractive and carefully groomed. He is between thirty and forty, of medium height and weight. His hair is light brown, neatly brushed and parted in the middle; his mustache and eyes are also brown. He dresses in the fashion of the day, obviously attentive to current style.

Two less apparent qualities of Gouvernail's appearance, however, hint at important traits of his character: his "penetrating" eyes and his remarkable white hands. Gouvernail, we soon find out, possesses a perceptive and delicate sensibility. After he spends just one hour with Athénaise, he knows her better than she knows herself. Not what she says, but, rather, what she half says allows the journalist to see her nature clearly. Her omissions and incompletions are interpreted by Gouvernail's "quick intelligence": "He knew that she adored Montéclin, and he suspected that she adored Cazeau without being herself aware of it. He had gathered that she was self-willed, impulsive, innocent, ignorant, unsatisfied, dissatisfied." To the reader, who has recently heard Athénaise complain that she detests living with Cazeau, having him "always there; his coats an' pantaloons hanging in [her] room; his ugly bare feet—washing them in [her] tub, befo' [her] very eyes, ugh!," Gouvernail's observation about Athénaise's adoration of Cazeau comes as an unexpected revelation. Gouvernail begins to become the story's mature center of intelligence; his opinions and insights often simultaneously surprise and direct us.

Gouvernail soon finds Athénaise "the most beautiful woman he had ever seen." Although he usually joins the New Orlean's intellectual coterie on Sunday afternoons and evenings, he begins neglecting this routine in order to serve Athénaise and spend time with her. He secretly hopes that someday he will be able "to hold her with a lover's arms."

Gouvernail's morality in some ways appears far more liberal than that of a Cazeau, a Léonce Pontellier, or, even, a Robert Lebrun. He is like the intellectuals in the American quarter who are his associates—"*des esprits forts,* all of them . . . whose opinions would startle even the traditional 'sapeur,' for whom 'nothing is sacred.'" He tolerates married people, but generally looks upon marriage with deep suspicion. Gouvernail professes to feel no guilt about being attracted to a married woman. "That [Athénaise] was married," we learn, "made no particle of difference to Gouvernail. He could not conceive or dream of it making a difference. When the time came that she wanted him,—as he hoped and believed it would come,—he felt he would have a right to her."

However, underneath Gouvernail's liberal attitude toward the institution of marriage lies a rigorous and demanding morality. One night he finds Athénaise crying as she watches the toads hopping on the damp flagstones, crying because she is "heart-sick, body-sick." Gouvernail wants to embrace her, to strain her body against his own, to seek her lips. Desire and temptation grow fierce. Yet, Gouvernail fights to control his passion, for he believes that until Athénaise feels for him what he feels for her, he dare not act. According to Gouvernail's ethic, affection and longing must be mutual in order for a relationship to be satisfying and "moral." Because the newspaper writer senses that Athénaise perceives him only as a temporary replacement for her brother Montéclin, he forces himself to bridle his passion: "So long as she did not want him, he had no right to her,—no more than her husband had. It was very hard to feel her warm breath and tears upon his cheek, and her struggling bosom pressed against him and her soft arms clinging to him and his whole body and soul aching for her, and yet to make no sign."

Gouvernail suffers for loyalty to his gentleman's code. Athénaise, who has discovered that she is bearing Cazeau's child, quickly and eagerly decides to return to her husband. We readers, like Montéclin, cannot help but think that "the affair had taken a very disappointing, an ordinary, a most commonplace turn, after all." We are genuinely disappointed. We prefer Gouvernail in many ways to Cazeau. But Athénaise chooses sweeping sugar plantations and fidelity, nonetheless. And Gouvernail is left alone. He kindly takes her to the train station and buys her a ticket. There, he presses her hand warmly, as a father might, politely lifts his hat to her, and turns away. "He was a man of intelligence, and took defeat gracefully; that was all." As he heads back to his carriage, however, his thoughts reveal his depression. "By heaven, it hurts, it hurts!," he concludes. The code he lives by is not an easy one.

As we return to *The Awakening,* then, we bring to the novel special and important information about Chopin's New Orleans journalist. For example, we know that Gouvernail is a good-looking man who admires beautiful women; that he is keenly observant, with a quick, sensitive mind—at times a story's moral and intellectual center; that he knows and cherishes the works of great poets and relies on poetic omissions to supply truths inappropriate to utter; and that he has a very liberal attitude about extramarital relationships, tempered by a demanding moral code. We know Gouvernail is worth watching as wine and food are passed around Edna's dinner table.

Chopin introduces readers of *The Awakening* to Gouvernail with only a brief comment: "[Miss Mayblunt] had come with a gentleman by the name of Gouvernail, connected with one of the daily papers, of whom nothing special could be said, except that he was observant and seemed quiet and inoffensive." Readers of Chopin's other stories in which Gouvernail appears, however, recognize the understatement present in Chopin's casual comment. Gouvernail, we know, is *very* special: we have seen his silences and keen observations contributing significantly to meaning in other stories. During what appear to be quiet pauses and lapses in conversation, Gouvernail is often exhausting himself in thought. His mind is never still, though his lips may be; it works naturally and energetically to analyze people, relationships, and densely complex situations. We have watched him sense more, in a quiet way, about Mrs. Baroda and Athénaise than they are able to sense about themselves. We know his thoughts and reactions deserve our trust and greatest respect.

For instance, in the two lines from Swinburne that Gouvernail "murmurs" under his breath as the party progresses, we must suspect the kind of sensitive insight to character and action which we have seen before in similar comments. We immediately notice Gouvernail's intelligence at work as he selects lines that mention, precisely, the dominant colors of Edna's festive celebration: red and gold. "'There was a graven image of Desire /

Painted with red blood on a ground of gold,' " he utters. The lines perfectly recreate the color mood of the night. They recall the golden glimmer of Edna's gown, the yellow satin cover under strips of lacework on her table, and the yellow silk shades of her candelabra. They remind us of the full red and yellow roses in vases, roses Mrs. Highcamp weaves into a garland to place atop Victor Lebrun's handsome head.

But more than Gouvernail's knowledge of poetry and sensitivity to color is revealed by his recitation of lines from "A Cameo." Although Gouvernail has not been actively engaged in the frivolity of the night, he has been watching others behave impulsively, foolishly, recklessly. He is aware. Edna's passion is frequently the subject of concern among readers and critics of *The Awakening,* but in chapter 30 the issue of passion in general and its manifestations is central. "A Cameo," as the lines Gouvernail quotes begin to suggest and those he omits even more strongly imply, proposes the thesis that Desire can be destructive and ugly. On the beautiful gold ground there is engraved an image in blood. By Desire sit both "Pain" and "Pleasure." Not only Pain, but also Pleasure seems unattractive. Pleasure sits by his companion "with gaunt hands that grasped their hire." The tableau shows, also, "The senses and the sorrows and the sins, / And the strange loves" that follow like ugly beasts, wings and fins flapping. Like the tableau in the sonnet, there is something unpleasant, almost perverse about the scene in chapter 30. And Gouvernail recognizes it. Mrs. Highcamp, a middle-aged married woman, is drawn to Victor Lebrun in what seems a very unhealthy sense. She gives all of her attention to Victor at dinner, and waits for the chance to "reclaim his attention" after he turns for a moment to the prettier Mrs. Merriman. She transforms Edna's party into a Dionysian ritual as she crowns Victor with roses (his cheeks turn the color of crushed grapes!) and drapes a white scarf around his neck and shoulders. We know that when Mrs. Highcamp asks Victor to call on her daughter, her request is not without double motive: Mrs. Highcamp, herself, needs to see Victor again.

And it is not only Mrs. Highcamp who is aroused. Mrs. Merriman and even Miss Mayblunt, a woman thought by many to be "intellectual," a woman some even suspected "wrote under a *nom de guerre,*" are unsettled by the vision of young Victor Lebrun. Miss Mayblunt loses herself "in a rhapsodic dream" as she stares at him. Mrs. Merriman leans over Victor's elegant, regal-looking chair, grasps his glass, and holds it to his lips until he drains the last sip. She finally wipes his lips sensuously with her sheer handkerchief. Gouvernail's lines, spoken too softly for others in the room to even hear, express the confusion of the scene and suggest the danger of lust of this sort. Gouvernail, who had been able to control his desire for Athénaise, recognizing the ugly possibilities of not doing so, refuses to approve of what he sees. He seems to sense, once more, the futility and perversity of passion that lacks intimacy and affection. Koloski suggests that Gouvernail knows still more, something that has broad implications for the entire novel: "behind the sometimes wild activities of the guests is the brooding presence of death." Death, who stands "behind a gaping grate" in "A Cameo," not unlike Bergman's Death in *The Seventh Seal,* establishes the general mood of the novel and hints at Edna's fate. But Death also seems particularly and inextricably linked to the sort of Desire Swinburne's figures and the women in chapter 30 of *The Awakening* display.

Although the lines Gouvernail quietly utters at Edna's party remind us briefly of the "old" Gouvernail in "Athénaise" and "A Respectable Woman," we might still be somewhat surprised by his relatively minor role. This diminution of his once sizable role in earlier stories is significant. It not only dramatically draws attention to the Swinburne passage he does recite, but also adds an ironically pessimistic detail to a work full of a thousand dark ironies. For here, after all, is a man who might answer so many of Edna's needs. He has the courage to flaunt convention that Robert lacks, the spirit of adventure Léonce seems never to have possessed, and the respect for women Alcée Arobin only pretends to feel. And yet, on this night, in this novel, he has been primarily assigned the role of an ordinary dinner guest rather than philosopher / lover. For the first time, Chopin gives him a truly minor role. Chopin, we might guess, no longer believed in Gouvernail's idealistic love—nor in Edna's. The growing cynicism of Gouvernail and despair of Edna is what Chopin chooses *The Awakening* to register. Chopin silences this one man in the universe of her art who has previously shown himself as idealistic about the possibility of a happy and complete physical and spiritual union as Edna. Indeed, his progression from sensual bachelor ("A Respectable Woman") to disappointed lover ("Athénaise") to love cynic (*The Awakening*) has not been unlike Edna's progression recorded in the pages of *The Awakening*. Shortly after Gouvernail's single cynical observation during the Victor Lebrun incident, the quiet journalist says good night and disappears from Chopin's canon forever.

Kate Chopin's fiction presents a number of professional men who appear in more than one work: Friedheimer is the storekeeper in both "At the 'Cadian Ball" and "The Storm"; Lawyer Paxton manages legal matters in "Madame Célestin's Divorce," "Tante Cat'rinette," and "Dead Men's Shoes"; Dr. Bonfils attends to the sick and offers medical advice in "The Benitous' Slave" and "Beyond the Bayou." The reappearance of such professionals in work after work gives Chopin's central and southern Louisianan communities continuity and credibility. The stories maintain artistic auton-omy and yet appear strangely related to one another. We grow to welcome Chopin's professionals as neighbors—are always genuinely glad to see them—and enjoy the comfortable, reassuring sense of the familiar that they supply.

Throughout the stories in which he appears, Gouvernail highlights themes, establishes moods, and indicates, in subtle ways, the direction of Chopin's art and philosophy. We think about Gouvernail after we close *The Awakening*. We secretly hope to find him again in later stories: "A December Day in Dixie," "The Gentleman from New Orleans," "Charlie," "The Wood-Choppers," "Polly," and so on. But Chopin's decision to exclude him from her later fiction—primarily the fiction of happy endings—was the right one. He does not belong there. We have seen his cynicism increase. He remains for us, always, a man who must live by "the primordial fact of existence" he had discovered: "things seemed all wrongly arranged in this world, and no one was permitted to be happy in his own way."

JOYCE C. DYER

Kate Chopin's Sleeping Bruties

Kate Chopin's fiction is full of sleeping beauties, full of women who are
awakened by a man's glance or touch. Mildred Orme, Diantha, Caline, Zo-
raide, Mrs. Baroda, Athénaise, Fedora, Calixta, and—of course—Edna Pontellier all discover, through contact with men, that their passions have been
asleep, if not unborn. Diantha, for example, turns pale and quivers when a
summer painter kisses her good-bye at the season's end. Mildred Orme,
seated in "the snuggest corner" of the Kraummer's porch at the beginning
of "A Shameful Affair," finds a workman's violent kiss the most "delicious"
thing she has known in her twenty years of life. Mrs. Baroda, half-listening
to her husband's friend Gouvernail as he recites sensuous lines from Whitman, is confused and excited by the visitor's physical presence: "She wanted
to draw close to him and whisper against his cheek—she did not care what—
as she might have done if she had not been a respectable woman." And, as
we know, Edna is never the same after the erotic kiss of Alcée Arobin. "It
was the first kiss of her life to which her nature had really responded. It was
a flaming torch that kindled desire."

However, not only Chopin's women slumber and awake. The recent
popularity of *The Awakening* has given many the idea that Chopin is a
woman who writes best about women and their nature. But a review of
several of her best, though little-known, short stories indicates that she recognized and understood the passions and needs of men as well as women,
of (humorously speaking) sleeping "bruties" as well as beauties. Indeed, in

From *The Markham Review* 10 (Fall/Winter 1980–81). © 1981 by Wagner College.

"Azélie" (written July 22–23, 1893), "At Chênière Caminada" (written October 21–23, 1893) and "A Vocation and a Voice" (written in November 1896) the protagonists are men who are sexually awakened and aroused by the soft skin, magical voices, or disturbing and mysterious personalities of women. Chopin records the awakenings of 'Polyte, Tonie, and Brother Ludovic with symbolic care and controlled attention. As these stories and others suggest, her true subject was both men and women. Her true subject was human nature.

In "Azélie," 'Polyte, Mr. Mathurin's storekeeper, lives his life with great concern for order and security. For example, he always carries the store key and a pistol in his back pocket during the day; at night he routinely places the key, the pistol, and his watch under his pillow. 'Polyte is careful to fasten the store's double wooden shutters and to lock the heavy door at the end of each day. He even protects his own private sleeping-room at the back of the store from potential discomfort. 'Polyte screens his windows and doors and plants a thick curtain of Madeira vines between the two pillars facing his room.

But there is one force that 'Polyte cannot protect himself against: his desire for a woman, for Azélie Pauché. Azélie, whose presence arouses 'Polyte in strange and unfamiliar ways, threatens the calm orderliness of 'Polyte's existence. He initially responds to her—to this incomprehensible threat—with anger, bewilderment, and exasperation. When Azélie appears at planter Mathurin's store one day, for example, 'Polyte says hurriedly, "Well, w'at you want, Azélie? I ain't got time to fool. Make has'e; say w'at you want." Azélie's calm reply, something about the need for a small piece of meat, distresses and puzzles 'Polyte. He scolds her: "Bonté! w'at you all do with meat yonda?" As Azélie continues to let her eyes wander over the shelves for further supplies, 'Polyte stares at her "with a sense of aggravation that her presence, her manner, always stirred up in him." 'Polyte finally fills Azélie's order, though, significantly, he forbids her those items that he thinks demoralizing: whiskey and tobacco. "No! Once fo' all, no!" 'Polyte cries as he refuses Azélie a dram of liquor for her father Arsene. After Azélie leaves the store, 'Polyte watches her with a "perplexed expression" on his face. A few minutes later, he urges Mr. Mathurin to stop giving credit to the Pauchés. But he cannot dismiss the matter with a "good-natured shrug," as his employer can. "I wish they was all back on Li'le river," 'Polyte mutters as he walks slowly away.

Throughout "Azélie," Chopin symbolically hints that although 'Polyte fears his instincts and is confused by them, he will not be able to avoid them. They are as real, ever-present, vital, and natural as the moonlight that so

often streams into this Chopin story. The moonlight literally and symbolically illuminates "Azélie": always in the background or foreground, the light
of the moon reminds us of the disturbing power of the woman-mystery.
Chopin raises Azélie herself to the level of a mythic figure, a kind of moon
Goddess who personifies the woman-mystery, by describing Azélie's physical
resemblances to the moon. Even her face, "colorless but for the red, curved
line of the lips," and hair, "plastered smooth back from the forehead and
temples" suggest the moon. And Azélie, like Lawrence's Anna Brangwen, is
forever moonlit. Wherever she walks, shafts of light trail obediently at her
heels or enfold her. When Azélie first enters 'Polyte's dark, shuttered store,
for example, "A broad ray of light streamed in . . . illuminating the dingy
interior." Later in the story, as 'Polyte lies in his hammock thinking about
Azélie, the moon creeps up, "a keen, curved blade of light above the dark
line of the cotton-field." 'Polyte cannot avoid contact with the moon, just as
he cannot avoid his impulses, desires, and biological drives.

The time comes, as the moonlight forecasts, when 'Polyte must admit
that his desire for Azélie is overpowering and inescapable. After 'Polyte
catches Azélie stealing, he can no longer dismiss his new feelings. Standing,
appropriately, in a pale beam of moonlight, 'Polyte and Azélie argue. 'Polyte
violently grasps her arm and accuses her of being a thief but gradually softens
and agrees to give her whatever supplies she wishes in the future. After she
leaves, 'Polyte hurries to once more secure the store. However, locks no longer
reassure him: "overcome by some powerful feeling that was at work within
him, he buried his face in his hands and wept." Strangely, her theft begins
to excite him and increase his desire. He now finds her supremely attractive.
'Polyte recognizes that he wants Azélie, even though his attraction to her
fills him with shame and disgust. "The very action of stealing which should
have revolted him had seemed, on the contrary, to inflame him with love.
He felt that love to be a degradation—something that he was almost ashamed
to acknowledge to himself; and he knew that he was hopelessly unable to
stifle it." 'Polyte shudders with disgust "to discern in [Azélie] a being so
wholly devoid of moral sense." And yet, as Robert Arner notes, perhaps
excitement accompanies his disgust because he thinks that Azélie, having
broken one social taboo, may break another—"the one concerning virginity
and chastity."

'Polyte does not know how to manage his new emotions. The "gnawing
want" he feels is so urgent that he often leaves his work to wander toward
her cabin. He kisses and caresses Azélie whenever she will permit him to do
so; he invents excuses just "to touch her hand with his." Later in the season,
however, 'Polyte tries to give his lust a publicly acceptable form. 'Polyte asks

Azélie to marry him. But she rejects his proposal. "I ain't goin' to stay yere wid you, Mr. 'Polyte," she boldly announces. "I'm goin' yonda on Li'le river wid my popa."

Moonstruck, 'Polyte can no longer function rationally. Instinct now rules. Normally a busy, industrious man who always keeps the shelves "well-lined," 'Polyte can accomplish little after Azélie departs. He goes to Mr. Mathurin, explaining that he can no longer serve as his storekeeper and that he wishes to quit. "W'at in the name o' sense are you talking about, 'Polyte!" Mr. Mathurin exclaims in reply. But, of course, the moonblind 'Polyte no longer talks "sense." When Mr. Mathurin requests a further explanation, 'Polyte, awkwardly beating his leg with his felt hat, replies, "I reckon I jus' as well go yonda on Li'le river—w'ere Azélie." The mysterious power of Woman—the power Azélie and the moon represent—has made 'Polyte a creature not only Mr. Mathurin but also 'Polyte himself cannot fully understand. 'Polyte has no choice but to follow his impulses. He must go to the river where Azélie now lives. He must be near the moon-faced girl.

In "At Chênière Caminada," Antoine Bocaze (known to the islanders as "Tonie") experiences a sexual awakening certainly as powerful as 'Polyte's. Tonie's awakening, like 'Polyte's, begins with new, though disguised, emotions for a woman. The early phases of Antoine's awakening, however, are marked by sentimentality and juvenile idealization rather than the confusion and anger of 'Polyte's initial feelings for Azélie. In section 1, Chopin describes Tonie's romantic feelings for Claire Duvigné, his Azélie figure. After hearing her play the church organ with emotion and skill, Tonie imagines that the organist must be an angel, must be a fair celestial being. His eyes explore her nut-brown hair and Leghorn sailor-hat. Returning to his modest home late Sunday evening, he dreamily informs his mother that he has been walking, walking he knows not where. Tonie can offer his mother no news or gossip, for his daydreams have made him inattentive to village conversations. After Tonie's mother tells him the organist's name, he can think of nothing else. Unable to eat his courtbouillon, Tonie foolishly continues to ponder the pleasantness of Claire's name. "Claire Duvigné; that is a pretty name. Don't you think so, mother? I can't think of anyone on the Chênière who has so pretty a one, nor at Grand Isle, either, for that matter. And you say she lives on Rampart Street?"

But Chopin assures us, directly, that Tonie's new feelings are an issue of sexual need rather than childish infatuation. Early the next morning, Tonie gets lame Philbert to repair his boat and sails to Grand Isle to watch Claire Duvigné. He seems to have no choice but to go. "He did not at first recognize this powerful impulse that had, without warning, possessed itself of his entire being," comments Chopin. But he obeys it automatically, even though he does not recognize what it is. He obeys it as he would "the dictates of hunger and thirst." Tonie spends most of the summer at Grand Isle following Claire secretly about. He watches her swim. He wants to see her open her bare, porcelain arms to meet and embrace the sea. And he follows her mechanically, unthinkingly, to the oaks, under which he plays croquet with the children.

But Chopin also assures us symbolically, as she does in "Azélie," that there are natural forces within each man that he cannot resist. Even Antoine's physical appearance and social behavior suggest the presence of primitive forces that must and will find expression. Physically, he seems half-animal, half-man. He possesses an equine face characteristic of Satyrs and Silens, a face "too long and bronzed." With "limbs too unmanageable," Tonie walks like a plodding, stumbling beast. At one point Claire Duvigné notices that he appears "as strong as an ox." And Tonie's social graces are as unrefined as those of the animals that Chopin associates him with. He is dumb in a crowd of people. He does not know how to talk to women: "He felt that he could speak intelligibly to no woman save his mother." Tonie fishes and sleeps and eats: his pleasures are simple. But in addition to describing Tonie's primitive appearance and ways, Chopin offers a metaphor from nature that emphasizes the urgency and power of his impulses. The first day Tonie arrives on Grand Isle in search of Claire is carefully described:

> The day was bright and beautiful with soft, velvety gusts of wind blowing from the water. From a cluster of orange trees a flock of doves ascended, and Tonie stopped to listen to the beating of their wings and follow their flight toward the water oaks whither he himself was moving.

The flight of the birds orchestrates Tonie's own flight. Like the birds who obey their instincts to fly, Tonie obeys his instinct to possess Claire. The impulses of the birds are so urgent that Tonie can hear "the *beating* of their wings." Later, we find that under Tonie's calm, rude exterior, "a man's heart was *beating* clamorously" (my italics). For both Tonie and the birds, the word *beating* suggests the strength and force of instinct. And, finally, we note that the birds and Tonie head toward the oaks, trees Chopin uses throughout her canon to represent the protective and biological nature of woman.

In section 3, Tonie's reason, as we might expect from early descriptions of his appearance and behavior, yields to "the savage instinct of his blood." But perhaps because Tonie is a simple, primitive, rather dull and rough man, the guilt that he feels about his passion is less conscious, and the violence that he displays is more extreme and perverse than the guilt and violence of 'Polyte. To Tonie—all his life an islander and fisherman, a man who lost his father in a Baratarian Bay squall—the sea has always represented extreme power. After Claire hires Tonie's small boat with a red lateen-sail, Tonie watches her with "shifting glances." He vaguely recognizes that he wants to possess and consume her in as violent a way as the sea has possessed and consumed his father. Indeed, notes Chopin, Claire knows nothing of "the full force and extent" of his desire. A church bell (appropriately) causes Tonie's reason to return temporarily: the Angelus bell that Tonie has heard ring all of his life reminds Tonie of the church's moral code and expectations. Indeed, Claire "was again that celestial being whom our Lady of Lourdes had once offered to his immortal vision." Nevertheless, although guilt and conscience momentarily restrain him, Tonie soon returns to his violent fantasies. After assisting Claire out of his boat, "He was stirred by a terrible, an overmastering regret, that he had not clasped [Claire] in his arms when they were out there alone, and sprung with her into the sea." Tonie now both physically and emotionally resembles Poseidon, the horse-god of the deep, who produced monstrous progeny. Tonie, Chopin tells us, "resolved within himself that if ever again she were out there on the sea at his mercy, she would have to perish in his arms. He would go far, far out where the sound of no bell could reach him." Oddly, "There was some comfort for him in the thought."

Tonie, unlike 'Polyte, is conveniently saved from the pain and confusion of wanting to possess a woman who can never be his. In section 4, Tonie discovers that Claire Duvigné has died. It is true that Tonie's reaction to Claire's death (he was glad for she was in heaven, where she belonged) has been found artistically awkward by some critics. George Arms, for example, feels that the realism of Tonie's portrait is undercut by his final remarks and claims that "the author asks the reader to share [Tonie's] view" about an afterlife. But Tonie's reaction, which successfully emphasizes his consuming desire to possess Claire, is quite consistent with his earlier portrait. Tonie's reaction is not meant to confirm our belief in an afterlife, but rather to convince us of the perversity of Tonie's jealous passion. It is better, he implies, to have Claire dead than with a man other than himself.

The unnamed boy in "A Vocation and a Voice" develops and "awakens" over a period of years. His awakening is far better-detailed than 'Polyte's or Tonie's, though it includes many stages one or both of the previous stories describe: the protagonist is at first seen as innocent or sexually naive; he experiences new, confusing sensations; he directly confronts his own eroticism; he feels guilty and tries to disguise or sublimate his passion; he yields to his overpowering instinct. "A Vocation and a Voice" is a twenty-six page story that James E. Rocks calls "a miniature bildungsroman." In it, a nameless boy emerges gradually into a post-Darwinian man.

As an early scene in Woodland Park indicates, the boy understands little about natural force at the start of the story, just as 'Polyte and Tonie understand little about natural instinct as their respective stories begin. For example, the boy thinks that nature is gentle, and he remains for some time oblivious to its driving insistence. After the young lad (who still speaks with a girlish treble voice) discovers that he has taken the wrong street car and finds himself in a park, far away from the grime and noise of his city home in "The Patch," he grows content watching nature. He observes a soft breeze playing fantastic games with fallen leaves, follows the bluish smoke from a smoldering leaf pile as it weaves itself between the birches, and dwells upon "the russet splendor of the Autumn foliage." The boy naively believes that nature is semi-divine—sublime and good. He becomes blessedly tranquil in its presence. He wonders "if Heaven might not be something like this." As he turns to leave the park, the boy vows to ask Father Doran to help him find work somewhere in the country, "somewhere that he might breathe as freely and contentedly as he had been doing for the past hour here in Woodland Park." The boy's response to nature is clearly the innocent response of a child.

After he agrees to travel with Suzima and Gutro, two vagabonds who come to represent aspects of the buried life (namely, sexual desire and violent tendencies), the boy begins to recognize "evil" but continues to believe, as 'Polyte does, that a good and careful person can lock it out. The boy, for instance, knows that his decision means having to endure Suzima's swearing and Gutro's uncouth behavior, but he thinks that evil and desire are external to himself, qualities in others that he can tolerate with indifference. The boy, then, is not shocked by Suzima's first words: "Damn [Gutro]." He has heard worse in "The Patch." Naively, the boy believes that his religious strength and good manners will keep his own speech gentle and refined. He does not swear himself; Father Doran has taught him self-control in catechism class. And Gutro's vileness the boy views with indifference, yet feels that such vileness cannot touch him. "His soul had passed through dark places untouched, just as his body was passing now, unharmed, through the night, where there were pitfalls into which his feet, some way, did not wander."

But the boy, as Chopin subtly suggests, is gradually losing some of his innocence: his instincts, like 'Polyte's and Tonie's, are becoming stronger and more troublesome. The boy is becoming increasingly bestial and violent.

He spends more and more time with the mules. When the boy first joins the vagabonds, Gutro does not permit him to touch or even think about his precious mules. After some time together, however, Gutro permits the boy to water and to care for them. In addition, Gutro teaches the boy to shoot and hunt, and occasionally they kill small animals together for feasts. With the boy's participation in male activities, Gutro's dirty stories begin to inflame rather than disgust him. "Some of them left the boy not so tranquil," the narrator understates.

But most of all, Suzima herself begins to anger and puzzle the boy as Azélie had angered and puzzled 'Polyte. "Within his very own soul—that part of him which thought, compared, weighing considerations—there was . . . disapproval [of Suzima]," notes Chopin. Once, invited to join a priest for dinner during the winter months the trio stayed in a village, the boy brings Suzima along and, reminded so keenly of the difference between the instinctive life and the reasoned life by the presence of the gypsy and the priest, gives her a vicious kick which suggests, "be quiet will you, and behave yourself in the company of your betters." Yet, although the priest tries to persuade the boy to remain with him (with reason, in other words), the boy cannot resist the charms of Suzima and the instinctive life. "I must go," he tells the priest. "I want to go," he adds resolutely. "A savage instinct stirred within [the boy]," comments Chopin, "and revolted against the will of this man who was seeking to detain him." After he leaves the village, he tries to read books which the village priest has given to him, but the sacred texts offer no explanation for his new feelings. Alone, the boy wanders about, "restless, expectant, looking for that which lured and eluded him, which he could not overtake."

As in "Azélie" and "At Chênière Caminada," Chopin symbolically equates the forces of human instinct with the forces of nature in order to demonstrate the power of her character's new feelings and forecast the inevitable failure of any attempt to combat them. Although the boy early on enjoys the beauty and peace of Woodland Park, as we have seen, even at this time nature is not really as gentle as the boy would like to think. Although their significance goes unrecognized, certain wanton and powerful impulses are present in nature. "The soft wind caressed him with a thousand wanton touches, and the scent of the earth and the trees [was]—damp, aromatic." And as the boy travels South with the gypsies, nature begins to stimulate him in new ways, to provide him with sensual rather than aesthetic and moral pleasure. The aroma, sounds, and feel of the country delight him. "He liked the scent of the earth and the dry, rotting leaves. . . . He liked the feel of the soft, springy turf beneath his feet when he walked, or of the rolling

pebbles when he mounted a stony hillside." Later in the story, as we will
see, Chopin continues to include metaphors from nature—ripening wheat,
for example—which remind us that man's impulses and nature's are much
the same, are equally urgent and insistent.

The boy, as Chopin's symbolism suggests, must one day discover how
strong his natural impulses are. His passion, like 'Polyte's and Tonie's, erupts
with unexpected intensity. Taking Gutro's mules to water one day, he observes Suzima sitting naked on a flat stone. Her image, surrounded by new
green plant growth, "ate into his brain and into his flesh with the fixedness
and intensity of white-hot iron." Significantly, when Suzima spots him she
cries out, "Oh! the devil!" The boy now experiences lust and, perhaps
through guilt, a feeling both 'Polyte and Tonie have also known, senses his
likeness to the devil as well as to God. His forehead beads with cold moisture.
Every inch of his skin prickles and burns as if he already stands in hell's
flames. "Every pulse in his body was beating, clamoring, sounding in his
ears like confused, distant drum-taps."

After the initial guilt and violence of his discovery, however, the boy,
unlike 'Polyte and Tonie, is temporarily able to experience mystical joy
through his sexual union with Suzima. He springs into Suzima's wagon and
lies rigid and faint beside her until she sweetly folds him in her arms and
holds him fast with her lips. The union mysteriously helps the boy care for
the world in a new way. "He seemed to have been brought in touch with
the universe of man and all things that live," writes the author. "He cared
more than ever for the creeping and crawling things, for the beautiful voice-
less life that met him at every turn; in sky, in rock, in stream, in the trees
and grass and flowers that silently unfolded the mysterious, inevitable existence." Indeed, through sex the boy seems to experience a kind of rebirth;
he discovers new contentment and new harmony. Suzima "had become something precious and apart from all things in the world. . . . She was the embodiment of desire and the fulfillment of life."

However, the boy soon recognizes that passion has many currents, many
directions. Instinctively wanting to protect Suzima from Gutro's abuse, the
boy lunges at the Beast with a hunting knife. And this new direction—the
unexplainable readiness of a man to kill to protect his own—frightens the
boy. "An overwhelming confusion of thoughts, fears, intentions crowded
upon him. He felt as if he had encountered some hideous being with whom
he was not acquainted and who had said to him: 'I am yourself.'"

Now fearful and guilty, the boy tries to hide from passion and violence.
Unlike Tonie, who conveniently avoids the consequences of passion through
Claire's death, the boy must find a way to manage his very strong emotions

which make him shrink from self-trust. Not surprisingly, he decides to devote the rest of his life to religion and God. His soul, the narrator observes, "turned toward the refuge of spiritual help, and he prayed to God and the saints and the Virgin Mary to save him and to direct him." He leaves Suzima, joins a holy order at a monastery, and takes the name "Brother Ludovic." Here, significantly, he tries to recover his earlier belief that the natural life can be one of complete contentment, godly devotion, and moral calm. His ordering of nature at the monastery reflects his desire for inner peace. He becomes a sort of naturalist, eager to seek God and peace in nature's wonders. He learns the names of every bird, tree, and rock in the vicinity: the other brothers view him as an heroic woodsman. Symbolically unwilling to accept the brutality and passion of nature and natural man, Brother Ludovic builds a wall around the "Refuge," a wall that will keep away "That hideous, evil spectre of himself lurking outside, ready at any moment to claim him should he venture within its reach."

But Brother Ludovic in section 12 must admit, as 'Polyte had admitted, that he has no choice, after all, but to follow the woman he desires. When Brother Ludovic recognizes Suzima's voice, he experiences almost exactly the same sensations that he had on the day that he had first seen Suzima naked by the stream—sensations that Chopin anticipates in her descriptions of the wild and reckless breeze, the ripe wheat that Brother Ludovic tries to avoid by gathering his skirt around his knees, and the "Azélie"-like moon that shines brightly when Suzima draws near. Indeed, for all his building and praying, his instincts and physical desires remain quite the same. "He knew now that he had pulses, for they were clamoring, and flesh, for it tingled and burned as if prickled with nettles," explains Chopin. The needs of Brother Ludovic's flesh are more imperative than those of his spirit. The ending, as Per Seyersted notes, leaves no doubt that "the protagonist [chooses] the flesh rather than the spirit." Brother Ludovic cannot fight his instincts, his need for physical contact with the woman. Conscious only of Suzima's voice, "He sprang upon the bit of wall he had built and stood there, the breeze lashing his black frock." The last sentence of the story very simply states that "Brother Ludovic bounded down from the wall and followed the voice of the woman." No more need be said.

These three stories illustrate something that readers of only *The Awakening* and a few of Chopin's better-known short stories (such as "A Shameful Affair," "A Respectable Woman," and "Athénaise") might naturally overlook: Chopin was interested in the passions and drives of man (her "brutes") as well as of woman (her "beauties"). Again and again, in articles, dissertations, and college classrooms, we hear the words "feminist" and "feminine point of view" attached to the name of Kate Chopin. But in the three stories considered here, as well as in many others ("At the 'Cadian Ball" [July 15–17, 1892], "In and Out of Old Natchitoches" [February 1–3, 1893], "A Morning Walk" [April, 1897], and "The Storm" [July 19, 1898], for example), Chopin seriously undertakes the exploration of male passion. Kate Chopin was fascinated by the basic, primitive desires of both men and women. Her point of view was not strictly feminine. Both males and females, she seems to tell us, are complex creatures who have no choice but to discover their passion, in spite of risks, confusion, and guilt.

ELAINE GARDINER

"Ripe Figs":
Kate Chopin in Miniature

One of the most charming pieces Kate Chopin ever wrote occupies only one page of *The Complete Works*. Originally published on August 19, 1893, in *Vogue* magazine and titled "Ripe Figs (An Idyll)," this short work was later reprinted in the second of Chopin's short story collections, *A Night in Acadie* (1897), without the parenthetical subtitle. "Ripe Figs" is not a story except in the most rudimentary sense; it barely qualifies as a sketch. But it charms and seduces the reader with its sensuality and form, and it compels multiple readings. This story deserves a wider audience; luckily, its brevity allows me to quote it in full before making further comments.

> Maman-Nainaine said that when the figs were ripe Babette might go to visit her cousins down on the Bayou-Lafourche where the sugar cane grows. Not that the ripening of figs had the least thing to do with it, but that is the way Mamam-Nainaine was.
>
> It seemed to Babette a very long time to wait; for the leaves upon the trees were tender yet, and the figs were like little hard, green marbles.
>
> But warm rains came along and plenty of strong sunshine, and though Maman-Nainaine was as patient as the statue of la Madone, and Babette as restless as a humming-bird, the first thing they both knew it was hot summer-time. Every day Babette danced out to where the fig-trees were in a long line against the

From *Modern Fiction Studies* 28, no. 3 (Autumn 1982). © 1982 by the Purdue Research Foundation.

fence. She walked slowly beneath them, carefully peering between
the gnarled, spreading branches. But each time she came discon-
solate away again. What she saw there finally was something that
made her sing and dance the whole long day.

When Maman-Nainaine sat down in her stately way to break-
fast, the following morning, her muslin cap standing like an au-
reole about her white, placid face, Babette approached. She bore
a dainty porcelain platter, which she set down before her god-
mother. It contained a dozen purple figs, fringed around with
their rich, green leaves.

"Ah," said Maman-Nainaine arching her eyebrows, "how early
the figs have ripened this year!"

"Oh," said Babette. "I think they have ripened very late."

"Babette," continued Maman-Nainaine, as she peeled the very
plumpest figs with her pointed silver fruit-knife, "you will carry
my love to them all down on Bayou-Lafourche. And tell your
Tante Frosine I shall look for her at Toussaint—when the chrysanthemums are in bloom."

Part of the charm of this sketch is its brevity and its simplicity of plot
and sensibility; part is its delineation of a people and a place, its Local Color
atmosphere; and part is its delicate sensory description. "Ripe Figs" does
not interest solely for these qualities, however, no matter how charmingly
achieved. For in its scant three hundred words, Chopin uses some techniques
common to much of her work, techniques which culminate in her masterpiece, *The Awakening*. Three of these techniques are her use of contrasts,
her use of natural imagery, and her cyclical plotting pattern.

Contrasts abound in *The Awakening*: the meadow with the sea, New
Orleans with Grand Isle, childhood with adulthood, innocence with experience, Edna with Adèle, Edna with Madame Reisz, Robert with Mr. Pontellier, Robert with Alcée, motherhood with artisthood, confinement with
space, waking with sleeping, duty with freedom, and life with death. One
could go on, but this list suffices to illustrate the centrality of contrasts in
this remarkable novel.

Contrasts are central to "Ripe Figs" also: Maman-Nainaine and Babette, youth and age, patience and impatience, innocence and experience,
exuberance and staidness, spring and summer, summer and fall, figs and
chrysanthemums—and again, I could go on. Without these contrasts, the
story would lose rhythm and purpose, for contrasts are at the heart of Chopin's syntax, as well as of her theme. For this is a world of slow yet certain

movement and change, not stasis. And yet the ironical beauty of Chopin's use of contrasts here is that they ultimately convey and emphasize continuity and stability. Unlike the contrasts in *The Awakening*, where opposites strive for dominance, the contrasts in "Ripe Figs" are in happy equilibrium, so that movement and stillness coexist and create the special appeal of the work.

Let me elaborate on a few of the contrasts. Maman-Nainaine and her goddaughter, Babette, are counterpoints. Though their ages are not specified, at least a generation seems to separate them, and the difference is that between youth and maturity. Babette is as "restless as a hummingbird"; Maman-Nainaine is as "patient as the statue of la Madone." Babette "dance[s]" as she goes to check the fig trees and "sing[s]" and "dance[s]" when she discovers they have ripened. Maman-Nainaine is "stately" and has a "placid face" as Babette approaches her with the platter of figs. Babette's is the energy that moves nature along, the "force that through the green fuse drives the flower"; Maman-Nainaine's is the tranquil energy of nature's continuity.

The seasons also contrast—the spring and summer of the story, the fall previewed in the final line, and the winter intimated in the story's movement. The sketch opens in the spring when the figs are "like little hard, green marbles" and closes in the summertime when they are "purple" and "fringed around with their rich, green leaves." But though the actual closing occurs in the summer, the reader is left with a vision of fall—"when the chrysanthemums are in bloom," as Maman-Nainaine entrusts Babette with her message for Tante Frosine. The reader supplies the next seasonal reference, a winter marker of some kind, and the contrasts continue—and with them, movement. The figs and chrysanthemums are emblems of the seasons, markers that signal changes in people's lives, but changes here that are not so much changes as repetitions.

A second technique common to most of Chopin's work is the use of natural images—as emotional correlatives, as symbols, and as structural parameters. This use of natural images accounts, in part, for Chopin's early reputation as a Local Colorist and for her enduring reputation as a masterful evocator of place.

In "Ripe Figs," natural images are paramount. Not only are journeys planned according to when figs ripen and chrysanthemums bloom, but places are defined by what they produce; thus, Bayou-Lafourche, for Maman-Nainaine, is the place "where the sugar cane grows." The story is tightly structured between these natural boundaries, both temporal and spatial. It is these that give such movement as there is to the work. For both Babette and Maman-Nainaine wait on natural changes, one by natural inclination, the other by familial directive. And for this reason, most of the piece describes the progress of nature: "the leaves upon the trees were tender yet, and the figs were like little hard, green marbles"; "warm rains came along and plenty of strong sunshine"; the fig trees have "gnarled, spreading branches"; and the "purple figs" are "fringed around with their rich, green leaves."

This is not yet the rich symbolic imagery which structures *The Awakening*, though it does have the same unifying power. The figs and chrysanthemums are important, but other fruits and flowers might serve as well, given the same growing seasons, and they probably do serve Maman-Nainaine at other times.

Without being symbolic, however, these images are still correlatives for moments of readiness in people's lives. Babette is learning, through Maman-Nainaine's tutelage, to watch and to follow the seasons and nature's changes. "Not that," as the text tells us, "the ripening of the figs had the least thing to do with it," but because "that is the way Maman-Nainaine was." And it is probably the way Babette will be. In her childish exuberance and impatience, she studies the natural processes far more closely than Maman-Nainaine, so closely that for her the ripening of the figs is an excruciatingly slow process. For Maman-Nainaine, the natural process is compressed by her inattention; for Babette, it is extended by her scrutiny: "'Ah,' said Maman-Nainaine, arching her eyebrows, 'how early the figs have ripened this year!'" "'Oh,' said Babette, 'I think they have ripened very late.'" Babette's absorption with the natural changes that will herald the time of her visit to the Bayou-Lafourche becomes the reader's absorption, as the narrator directs our attention, with an almost surrealistic intensity, to the metamorphic maturation of the figs. Images of nature inform this sketch and give it charm, but not alone. It is the interplay among woman, child, and nature that charms, the casual reliance on natural patterns, not for any inherent meaning they may have, but just because they *are,* because "that is the way Maman-Nainaine [is]."

A final technique of "Ripe Figs" that recurs in Chopin's work, most notably in *The Awakening,* is the use of a cyclical pattern. Many of Chopin's stories end where they began, albeit not without significant change in the characters or their situations. *The Awakening* ends where it began—at Grand Isle, but it is a different Edna who walks into the sea than the Edna who walks up from the sea with Robert in the novel's opening. In "Ripe Figs," the change in Babette is much more subtle, nothing more significant than a couple of months' growth and a sense of observance and expectation rewarded. But the circular pattern of "Ripe Figs," unlike most other Chopin stories with this pattern, is unbroken at the end. For with the ripening of the figs in the summertime begins the next period of waiting, the continuance of the cycle, both of nature and of the characters' lives. Maman-Nainaine will travel to Toussaint in the fall, "when the chrysanthemums are in bloom." The reader finishes the sketch anticipating the movements to follow—movements directed by the seasons, by natural happenings, by the cyclical patterns of these people's lives. These patterns both imitate and anticipate nature's cycle until, with Yeats, we ask: "how can we know the dancer from the dance?"

SANDRA M. GILBERT

The Second Coming of Aphrodite

The radiant ancient Venus, the Aphrodite born from the white foam of the sea, has not traversed the horrifying darkness of the Middle Ages with impunity. . . . She has retired into the depths of a cave . . . lighted up by fires which are not those of the benign Phoebus.
—CHARLES BAUDELAIRE, "R. Wagner & Tannhaüser in Paris," 1861

> *Then to me so lying awake a vision*
> *Came without sleep over the seas and touched me,*
> *Softly touched mine eyelids and lips; and I too,*
> *Full of the vision,*
>
> *Saw the white implacable Aphrodite,*
> *Saw the hair unbound and the feet unsandalled*
> *Shine as fire of sunset on western waters*
> —A. C. SWINBURNE, "Sapphics," 1865

I was born under the star of Aphrodite, Aphrodite who was also born on the sea, and when her star is in the ascendant, events are always propitious to me.
—ISADORA DUNCAN, *My Life,* 1927

> *Swiftly re-light the flame,*
> *Aphrodite, holy name*
>
> . . . .
>
> *return, O holiest one,*
> *Venus whose name is kin*
>
> *to venerate,*
> *venerator.*
> —H. D., *Tribute to*
> *the Angels,* 1945

From *The Kenyon Review* 5, no. 3 (Summer 1983). © 1983 by Kenyon College.

Toward the end of Kate Chopin's *The Awakening* there is a dinner party scene which has been ignored by many critics though it has fascinated and puzzled a few. On the verge of leaving her husband's house for a nearby cottage that she hopes will become both a spiritual and material room of her own, Edna Pontellier has invited a "select" group of friends to join her at a birthday dinner which will also be a ceremonial celebration of her departure from one household and her entrance into another. Splendid in gold satin and lace "the color of her skin," she presides over an equally splendid table, which is similarly decked in "pale yellow satin," lit by "wax candles in massive brass candelabra," and heaped with "full, fragrant roses." More strikingly still, "the ordinary stiff dining chairs" have been "discarded for the occasion and replaced by the most commodious and luxurious which could be collected throughout the house" while "before each guest [stands] a tiny glass that [sparkles] like a garnet gem," containing a special, magical-looking cocktail. Enthroned at the head of the table, Edna herself appears equally magical, for there is "something in her attitude, in her whole appearance, which [suggests] the regal woman, the one who rules, who looks on, who stands alone." At the same time, however—even in the midst of gold champagne, crimson cocktails, and general merrymaking which climaxes in one of the women guests weaving a pagan garland of roses to crown the dark curls of the handsome young man beside her—we are told that Edna feels an "old ennui overtaking her . . . a chill breath that seemed to issue from some vast cavern wherein discords wailed," (chap. 30). Ranging as it does from sumptuous feasting to secret, inexplicable sadness, from gorgeousness to gloom, the dinner party chapter represents, as Cynthia Griffin Wolff observes, "one of the longest sustained episodes in the novel."

Perhaps it is because so many contemporary critics would agree with Lawrence Thornton's recent description of *The Awakening* as a "political romance" that so few have paid close attention to this scene. Though in the last decade *The Awakening* has become one of the most frequently taught and persistently analyzed American novels, commentators on the book commonly describe Edna's party, if they discuss it at all, as just one more occasion when Chopin's half-mad housewife experiences and expresses "unfocused yearning" for romantic transfiguration or social liberation. Besides occupying an exceptionally elaborate chapter in a novel of economical, obliquely rendered episodes, however, Edna's dinner party constitutes an extraordinarily complex literary structure, a scene whose images and allusions as well as its dramatic plot suggest surprisingly rich veins of symbolic significance. What does it mean, after all, when the narrator of this apparently "realistic" work suddenly calls her heroine "the regal woman, the one who rules, who looks on, who stands alone"? The vocabulary of such a description seems more appropriate to a fantasy, a romance, or a fairy tale, and yet this mysterious definition seems also to evoke the narrator's next perception of the "chill breath" her queenly heroine feels, together with Edna's corollary, equally mystical and mysterious sense of "acute longing which always summoned into her spiritual vision the presence of the beloved one." Who or what, indeed, is the oddly vague "beloved one"? And why, finally, does the enigmatically wise Mlle. Reisz take her leave of Edna with a French sentence—*"Bonne nuit, ma reine, soyez sage"*—that seems to confirm our feeling that this magical hostess is clothed in a paradoxical veil of power and vulnerability?

As a speculative explanation of these puzzles I want to argue that *The Awakening* is a female fiction that both draws upon and revises *fin de siècle* hedonism to propose a feminist and matriarchal myth of Aphrodite/Venus as an alternative to the masculinist and patriarchal myth of Jesus. In the novel's unfolding of this implicit myth, the dinner party scene is of crucial importance, for here, as she presides over a Swinburnian Last Supper, Edna Pontellier definitively (if only for a moment) "becomes" the powerful goddess of love and art into whose shape she was first "born" in the Gulf near Grand Isle and in whose image she will be suicidally borne back into the sea at the novel's end. Thus when Victor, the dark-haired young man who was ritually draped and garlanded at the climax of the feast, tells his friend Mariequita that "Venus rising from the foam could have presented no more entrancing a spectacle than Mrs. Pontellier, blazing with beauty and diamonds at the head of the board," he is speaking what is in some deep sense the truth about Kate Chopin's heroine.

To see *The Awakening* in these terms is not, of course, to deny that it is also the work most critics and readers have thought it is: a "Creole Bovary," a feminist "critique of the identity of 'mother-women,'" a New Orleans version of "the familiar transcendentalist fable of the soul's emergence, or 'lapse' into life," "a eulogy on sex and a muted elegy on the female condition," a turn-of-the-century "existentialist" epiphany, and "a tough-minded critique of the Victorian myths of love." Taken together, all of these definitions of the novel articulate the range of political, moral, and philosophical concerns on which Chopin meditates throughout this brief but sophisticated work. What unifies and dramatizes these often divergent matters, however, is the way in which, for all its surface realism, *The Awakening* is allusively organized by Kate Chopin's half-secret (and perhaps only half-conscious) but distinctly feminist fantasy of the second coming of Aphrodite.

To be sure, Chopin's "Creole Bovary" has always been understood to be, like its French precursor, a novel that both uses fantasy and comments upon fantasy in order to establish the character of its heroine and the nature of her character. From the severest early reviewers to the most enthusiastic recent writers, however, most critics see such fantasies as, like Emma Bovary's, symptoms of inadequacy, of an "over-idealization of love" and a "susceptibility to romantic codes." People like Edna Pontellier and Emma Bovary, wrote Willa Cather in 1899, "are the spoil of the poets, the Iphigenias of sentiment." Edna's commitment to fantasy, concludes Cynthia Griffin Wolff in a somewhat extreme summary of this position, is the ultimate mark of the "schizoid" personality which causes her "disintegration." I will argue, however, that the details of desire which the text of *The Awakening* records ultimately shape themselves into a tale of romantic transfiguration that not only uses and comments upon fantasy but actually becomes a fantasy, albeit a shadowy one. Both seriously and ironically this fantasy of Kate Chopin's shows, from a female point of view, just what would "really" happen to a mortal, turn-of-the-century woman who tried to claim for herself the erotic freedom and power owned by the classical queen of love.

I will argue, moreover, that to see this novel as such a shadowy fantasy or fantasy *manqué* is to begin to explain a number of qualities that have puzzled its severe critics as well as its enthusiastic admirers: its odd short chapters, its ambiguous lyricism (what Willa Cather called its "flexible iridescent style"), its editorial restraint, its use of recurrent images and refrains, its implicit or explicit allusions to writers like Whitman, Swinburne, Flaubert, and its air of moral indeterminacy. In addition, I will suggest more specifically that to see *The Awakening* as such a fantasy is to begin to grasp the purpose of some of the scenes in the book that have always appeared problematical—the often ignored or misrepresented episode of the dinner party, for example, and the even more controversial scene of Edna's suicide. Finally, I will show that in creating this realistically surfaced, generically equivocal fantasy, Kate Chopin was working in a mode of mingled naturalism and symbolism exactly analogous to the one explored by her near contemporary George Moore and his younger countryman James Joyce. Learned from such varied continental precursors as Turgenev and Balzac, Maupassant and Chekhov, this artful combination of surface and symbol evolved through Moore's *The Untilled Field* and Joyce's *Dubliners* to a famous culmination in *Ulysses*. But Kate Chopin in America, inheriting the same tradition and similar techniques, also began to give emphasis to the fantastic or mythic radiance that might at any moment flash through ordinary reality. Because she was female, however, she saw such epiphanies from a feminine point of view and in what we would now call feminist terms. Indeed, the next literary woman to employ the same mode and the same techniques would be Virginia Woolf, and she too would use them to valorize and mythologize femaleness.

Appropriately enough, Kate Chopin's portrait of Aphrodite as a Creole Bovary begins and ends at a seaside resort, on the margin between nature and culture, where a leisured or, anyway, a lucky few may be given (as only a few have always been given) the chance to witness the birth of erotic power in the foam. To start with, however, despite the nearness of the sea and the incessant sound of its "seductive" voice, Chopin offers scenes that seem determinedly realistic, low-key, landbound. In addition, as if briefly but formally acknowledging Flaubert's influence, she opens her novel about a woman's fateful transformation by examining her heroine from a solid and stolid male perspective. *Madame Bovary,* of course, begins with a brief summary of Charles Bovary's history, including a description of the way Emma Rouault looks to the bovine but passionate young physician whom she will soon marry. Similarly, *The Awakening*'s author-omniscient first chapter emphasizes the point of view of Edna Pontellier's conventional husband, Léonce.

Like Madame Bovary's husband-to-be, who at one point gazes at Emma as she stands beneath a parasol that colors "the white skin of her face with shifting reflections," Mr. Pontellier watches from a porch on the main building of Madame le Brun's Grand Isle summer colony as "a white sunshade [advances] at a snail's pace from the beach" with his wife Edna and her friend Robert Le Brun strolling "beneath its pink-lined shelter" (chap. 1). In both cases, the woman appears first as an object, and Edna in particular, whether she "is" herself or the walking sunshade that contains her, is presented as she seems to Léonce: valuable, even treasured, but nevertheless, a *thing* to be possessed and guarded rather than a person to be heard or heeded. Even this early in her novel, however, and even while acknowledging her debt to Flaubert, Chopin swerves from him by emphasizing this last point. For where the French novelist creates sympathy for Charles with his devastating portrait of the first Madame Bovary, a skinny pimpled Jocasta who is not only old enough to be the young doctor's mother but has actually been chosen for him by his mother, Chopin immediately characterizes Léonce as an impatient businessman who scrutinizes his wife for sunburn "as one looks at a valuable piece of personal property which has suffered some damage" (chap. 1).

Most of *The Awakening* is told from Edna's perspective, with occasional editorial interpolations from the narrator, but despite (or perhaps because

of) its unrepresentative point of view and its air of almost impressionistic
improvisation, this opening chapter constitutes a surprisingly complete introduction to the problems and personae of the novel. As an overture, in
fact, it includes many of the major leitmotifs of the work to follow: symbolic
objects (houses, clothing, jewelry, food); symbolic activities (piano playing,
swimming, housecleaning, gambling); symbolic figures, both human and inhuman (the birds, the lady in black, the twins, Edna and Robert, Mr. Pontellier, Madame Le Brun); symbolic places (the Gulf, the beach, the city, the
summer colony on Grand Isle), and crucial relationships (husbands and
wives, mothers and children). First encountered here, most of these ultimately extraordinary elements seem ordinary enough, or rather they seem as
vividly literal as objects in a painting by Renoir or Seurat. It is only as one
scene dissolves into another, as the narrative point of view gradually enters
Edna's strengthening consciousness, and as objects and activities insistently
recur, like elements of a protracted dream, that they begin to gain what
eventually becomes an almost uncanny power. Porches and pianos, mothers
and children, skirts and sunshades—all these are the props and properties
of domesticity, the key elements of what in the nineteenth century was called
"woman's sphere," and it is in this sphere, on the edge of a blue gulf, that
Edna Pontellier is securely caged when she first appears in the novel that will
tell her story. In a larger sense, however, she is confined in what is not only
literally a "woman's sphere" but, symbolically speaking, the Woman's
House—the place to which in civilized as in primitive cultures women are
ritually assigned at crucial times in their lives. Here, therefore, every object
and figure has not only a literal domestic function and a dreamlike symbolic
radiance but a distinctively female symbolic significance.

The self-abnegating "mother-women" who seem "to prevail that summer at Grand Isle," the mutually absorbed young lovers who always appear
in the neighborhood of the sepulchrally religious lady in black, Edna's own
children trailed by their omnipresent quadroon nurse with her "faraway,
meditative air," awkward and imperious Mademoiselle Reisz in her "rusty
black lace" and artificial violets, the Farival twins "always clad in the virgin's
colors," the skirt-dancing little girl in black tulle, even Edna herself sharing
out her husband's gift of *friandises*—all seem like faintly grotesque variations
on the figures from "La Vie D'une Femme" who appear in Charlotte Brontë's
Villette: the young girl, the bride, the mother, the widow. That the *pension*
in which all these women have gathered is ruled by the pretty but powerful
widow Madame Le Brun, who sews and oversees in a light airy room with
a view at the top of the house, seems quite appropriate. At the same time,
however, it seems quite appropriate that the novel begins with the comical

curse of the caged parrot—"*Allez vous-en! Allez vous-en! Sapristi!*"—and with the information that this same bird also speaks "a language which nobody understood, unless it was the mocking bird that hung on the other side of the door." For, as we shall see, these birds together prefigure both Edna's restlessness and her irony, her awakening desire for freedom and her sardonic sense that freedom may ultimately be meaningless, her yearning for solitude and her skeptical worries about loneliness.

Before these desires and fears become fully conscious, however, and even while it is slowly becoming clear that the domesticity of these early chapters is symbolically as well as literally important, Chopin begins to dramatize her heroine's summer of discontent through a series of traditionally "realistic" interactions between Edna and her husband. Indeed, though the technique and structure of these exchanges may be derived in part from French writers like Flaubert and Maupassant, they are most thematically indebted to the female literary tradition in English, of which Kate Chopin was surely an heir. Thus, depicting Léonce's casual self-absorption and Edna's mild rebelliousness, the narrator of *The Awakening* at first seems primarily concerned to represent with Austenian delicacy a marriage on the edge of Eliotian fissures. Pontellier is not, of course, either a Casaubon or a Grandcourt, but that seems in fact to be Chopin's revisionary point. For as she depicts both his power and his imperiousness in swift, understated domestic episodes—the scene in chapter 3 when he wakes Edna and the children, for instance, or his offhand gifts of money and *friandises*—she shows that he too is possessed by the possessive male will which speaks differently but equally in the tyrannical husbands of *Daniel Deronda* and *Middlemarch*. To begin with, therefore, Edna's "awakening" is both domestic and prosaic. Like Dorothea Brooke and Gwendolyn Harleth, she awakens from the romantic dreams of girlhood first to find herself a married woman and then to find that the meaning of marriage is very different from what she had supposed. Like another nineteenth-century heroine—Emily Brontë's Catherine Earnshaw Linton—she experiences what Chopin calls "an indescribable oppression" which seems to come at least in part from her sense of herself as, in Brontë's words, "the wife of a stranger; an exile, and outcast . . . from what had been [her] world." For when, like the subject of one of Emily Dickinson's poems, she rises to "His Requirements" and takes on "the honorable work of Woman and of Wife," she seems to have accepted a spiritual confinement that excludes all visions of "Amplitude and Awe."

For George Eliot's comparatively docile Dorothea and her chastened Gwendolyn, even for Emily Brontë's more satanically ambitious Catherine, such a recognition of domestic entrapment along with its corollary spiritual diminution is the climax of a long process of social reconciliation that must ultimately end in these heroines accepting their own comparative powerlessness. For Edna, on the other hand, this maritally-induced recognition of "her position in the universe as a human being, and . . . her relations as an individual to the world within and about her" (chap. 6) is only the beginning of a more metaphysical awakening to all the visionary intimations and implications of her own femaleness. To be sure, once she has left her husband's bed to sit on the porch and listen to "the everlasting voice of the sea," she has already, like Eliot's and Brontë's heroines, acquired what her author ironically calls "more wisdom than the Holy Ghost is usually pleased to vouchsafe to any woman." But, like Emily Dickinson, Chopin wants to record not only the body's rebellion at confinement but the soul's "moments of Escape," along with the visions that empower such escapes. In addition, because she is a fiction writer, she wants to create a narrative that will enact and record those visions. After her first, realistically rendered discoveries of spiritual uneasiness, therefore, Edna's "awakenings" become increasingly fantastic and poetic, stirrings of the imagination's desire for amplitude and awe rather than protests of the reason against unreasonable constraint.

Paradoxically, however, it is just Edna's realistic awakenings to domestic confinement and her domestic confinement itself that make possible these later, more visionary awakenings. Specifically, I would argue, Edna awakens to the possibilities as well as the problems of "her position in the universe" not only because she finds herself enclosed in woman's literal sphere and inhabiting a figurative House of Women but also because she has come to spend the summer in what is both literally and figuratively a female colony, a sort of parodic Lesbos. In fact, though not many critics have noticed this, Madame Le Brun's *pension* on Grand Isle is very much a woman's land, not only because it is owned and run by a single woman and dominated by "mother-women" but also because (as in so many summer colonies today) its principal inhabitants are actually women and children whose husbands and fathers visit only on weekends. No wonder, then, that, as Chopin observes, "that summer at Grand Isle [Edna] had begun to loosen a little the mantle of reserve that had always enveloped her" (chap. 7) and had begun to do so under "the influence" first of beautiful and sensual Adèle Ratignolle and, later, of more severe and spiritual Mlle. Reisz.

From the eighteenth century on, after all, middle-class women's culture has often been fragmented by the relegation of each wife to a separate household, by the scattering of such households to genteel suburbs, and by the rituals of politeness that codified visiting behavior and other interchanges between the ladies of these separate households. While husbands joined to work and play in a public community of men, women were isolated in private parlors or used, in brief stylized public appearances, as conspicuous consumers to signify their husbands' wealth. Only a few situations, most notably the girls' school and the summer hotel, offered the isolated lady any real chance to participate in an ongoing community of women, one based on extended experiences of intimacy with others of their own sex. And, as *The Awakening* shows, for married adult women of Edna Pontellier's age and class the quasi-utopian communal household of the vacation hotel must have offered a unique opportunity to live closely with other women and to learn from them. My use here of the word "colony" is, therefore, deliberately ambiguous. For if a summer colony like Madame le Brun's *pension* is, on the one hand, a place where women have been colonized—that is, dominated and confined by men who have conquered them—in another sense this female-occupied *pension* is a place where women have established a colony or encampment of their own, an outpost of the lively dream queendom that Charlotte Perkins Gilman called "Herland."

Finally, then, the punning phrase "the Bonds of Womanhood" that Nancy Cott wisely uses as the title of her historical study of American women is also useful here. For in this close-knit summer colony locks become links: bonds in the negative sense of "fetters" gradually give way to bonds in the positive sense of "ties." Given this transformation of bondage into bonding, moreover, it is inevitable that both Adèle Ratignolle, the antithetical "mother-woman," and Mlle. Reisz, the equally antithetical spinster/artist, facilitate Edna's passage into the metaphorically divine sexuality that is *her* fated and unique identity. Responding to Adèle's interrogations in chapter 7, for instance, Edna begins to formulate her sense of the desirous quest for significant desire that has shaped her life. Similarly, responding in chapter 9 to the implicit challenge posed by Mlle. Reisz's music, she becomes conscious that "the very passions themselves were aroused within her soul, swaying it, lashing it, as the waves daily beat upon her . . . body."

The oceanic imagery embedded in Chopin's description of Edna's response to Mlle. Reisz's music is neither casual nor coincidental; rather it suggests yet another agency through which Mme. Le Brun's predominantly female summer colony on Grand Isle awakens and empowers this Creole Bovary. For Chopin's Aphrodite, like Hesiod's, is born from the sea, and born specifically because the colony where she comes to consciousness is situated, like so many places that are significant for women, outside patriarchal culture, beyond the limits of the city where men make history, on one of those magical shores that mark the margin where nature intersects with culture. Here power can flow from outside, from the timelessness or from, in Mircea Eliade's phrase, the "Great Time" that is free of historical constraints; and here, therefore, the sea can speak in a seductive voice, "never ceasing, whispering, clamoring, murmuring, inviting the soul to wander for a spell in abysses of solitude; to lose itself in mazes of inward contemplation" (chap. 6).

It is significant, then, that not only Edna's silent dialogue with Mlle. Reisz but also her confessional conversation with Adèle Ratignolle incorporates sea imagery. Reconstructing her first childhood sense of self for her friend, Edna remembers "a meadow that seemed as big as the ocean" in which as a little girl she "threw out her arms as if swimming when she walked, beating the tall grass as one strikes out in the water" (chap. 7). Just as significantly she speculates that, as she journeyed through this seemingly endless grass, she was most likely "running away from prayers, from the Presbyterian service, read in a spirit of gloom by my father that chills me yet to think of." She was running away, that is, from the dictations and interdictions of patriarchal culture, especially of patriarchal theology, and running into the wild openness of nature. Even so early, the story implies, her quest for an alternative theology, or at least for an alternative mythology, had begun. In the summer of her awakening on Grand Isle, that quest is extended into the more formalized process of learning not to run but to swim.

Edna's education in swimming is, of course, obviously symbolic, representing as it does both a positive political lesson in staying afloat and an ambiguously valuable sentimental education in the consequences of getting in over one's head. More important, however, is the fact that swimming immerses Edna in an *other* element—an element, indeed, of otherness—in whose baptismal embrace she is mystically and mythically revitalized, renewed, reborn. That Chopin wants specifically to emphasize this aspect of Edna's education in swimming, moreover, is made clear by the magical occasion on which her heroine's first independent swim takes place. Following Mlle. Reisz's evocative concert, "someone, perhaps it was Robert [Edna's lover-to-be], thought of a bath at that mystic hour and under that mystic moon." Appropriately, then, on this night that sits "lightly upon the sea and land," this night when "the white light of the moon [has] fallen upon the world like the mystery and softness of sleep," the previously timid Edna begins for the first time to swim, feeling "as if some power of significant import had been given her" and aspiring "to swim far out, where no woman had swum before" (chap. 10). Her new strength and her new ambition are symbolically fostered by the traditionally female mythic associations of moonlight and water, as well as by the romantic attendance of Robert Le

Brun and the seemingly erotic "heavy perfume of a field of white blossoms somewhere near." At the same time, however, Chopin's description of the waves breaking on the beach "in little foamy crests . . . like slow white serpents" suggests that Edna is swimming not only with new powers but into a kind of alternative paradise, one that depends upon deliberate inversions and conversions of conventional theological images, while her frequent reminders that this sea is a *gulf* reinforce our sense that its waters are at least as metaphysical as those of, say, the Golfo Placido in Conrad's *Nostromo*. Thus, even more important than Edna's swim are both its narrative and its aesthetic consequences, twin textual transformations that influence and energize the rest of Chopin's novel. For in swimming away from the beach where her prosaic husband watches and waits, Edna swims away from the shore of her old life, where she had lingered for twenty-eight years, hesitant and ambivalent. As she swims, moreover, she swims not only toward a female paradise but out of one kind of novel—the work of Eliotian or Flaubertian "realism" she had previously inhabited—and into a new kind of work, a mythic/metaphysical romance that elaborates her distinctively female fantasy of paradisiacal fulfillment and therefore adumbrates much of the feminist modernism that was to come within a few decades.

In a literal sense, of course, these crucial textual transformations can be seen as merely playful fantasies expressed by Robert and Edna as part of a "realistically" rendered courtship. I am arguing, though, that they have a metaphorical intensity and a mythic power far weightier than what would appear to be their mimetic function, and that through this intensity they create a ghostly subtextual narrative that persists with metaphorical insistence from Edna's baptismal swimming scene in chapter 10 through her last, suicidal swim in chapter 39. For when Edna says "I wonder if any night on earth will ever again be like this one," she is beginning to place herself in a tale that comes poetically "true." Her dialogue with Robert, as the two return from their moonlit midnight swim in the Gulf, outlines the first premises of this story. "It is like a night in a dream," she says. "The people about me are like some uncanny, half-human beings. There must be spirits abroad tonight" (chap. 10). Robert's reply picks up this idea and elaborates upon it. It is "the twenty-eighth of August," he observes, and then explains, fancifully, that

> on the twenty-eighth of August, at the hour of midnight, and if the moon is shining—the moon must be shining—a spirit that has haunted these shores for ages rises up from the Gulf. With its own penetrating vision the spirit seeks some one mortal wor-

thy to hold him company, worthy of being exalted for a few hours
into realms of the semicelestials. His search has always hitherto
been fruitless, and he has sunk back, disheartened, into the sea.
But tonight he found Mrs. Pontellier. Perhaps he will never wholly
release her from the spell. Perhaps she will never again suffer a
poor, unworthy earthling to walk in the shadow of her divine
presence.

(chap. 10)

Fanciful as it seems, however, this mutual fantasy of Edna's and Robert's is
associated, first, with a real change in their relationship, and then, with a
real change in Edna. Sitting on the porch in the moonlight, the two fall into
an erotic silence that seems to be a consequence of the fiction they have
jointly created: "No multitude of words could have been more significant
than those moments of silence, or more pregnant with the first-felt throbbings
of desire" (chap. 10). And the next day, when Edna awakens from her night
of transformative dreaming, she finds herself "blindly following whatever
impulse moved her, as if she had placed herself in alien hands for direction,
and freed her soul of responsibility" (chap. 12).

The scenes that follow—Edna's waking of Robert in chapter 12, their
voyage in the same chapter to the Chênière Caminada, their attendance at
church in chapter 13, Edna's nap at Madame Antoine's cottage again in
chapter 13, and their return to Grand Isle in chapter 14—constitute a wistful
adult fairy tale that lies at the heart of this desirous but ultimately sardonic
fantasy. Journeying across the Gulf to Mass on the nearby island of Chênière
Caminada—the island of live oaks—Edna and Robert find themselves in the
Fellini-esque company of the lovers, the lady in black, and a barefooted
Spanish girl (apparently Robert's sometime girlfriend) with the allegorical
name of Mariequita. Yet despite all this company Edna feels "as if she were
being borne away from some anchorage which had held her fast, whose
chains had been loosening," and together with Robert she dreams of "pirate
gold" and of yet another voyage, this one to the legendary-sounding island
of "Grande Terre," where they will "climb up the hill to the old fort and
look at the little wriggling gold snakes and watch the lizards sun themselves"
(chap. 12). When she finally arrives at the "quaint little Gothic church of
Our Lady of Lourdes," therefore, she is not surprisingly overcome by "a
feeling of oppression and drowsiness." Like Mariequita, the Church of Our
Lady of Lourdes is named for the wrong goddess, and Edna inevitably struggles—as she did when "running away from prayers" through the Kentucky
meadow—to escape its "stifling atmosphere . . . and reach the open air."

Everything that happens after she leaves the church further implies that she has abandoned the suffocation of traditional Christian (that is, traditional patriarchal) theology for the rituals of an alternative, possibly matriarchal but certainly female religion. Attended by the ever-solicitous Robert, she strolls across the "low, drowsy island," stopping once—almost ceremonially—to drink water that a "mild-faced Acadian" is drawing from a well. At "Madame Antoine's cot," she undresses, bathes, and lies down "in the very center of [a] high, white bed," where like a revisionary Sleeping Beauty, she sleeps for almost a whole day. When she awakens, for the fifth or sixth but most crucial time in this novel of perpetual "awakening," she wonders, "How many years have I slept? . . . The whole island seems changed. A new race of beings must have sprung up . . . and when did our people from Grand Isle disappear from the earth?" (chap. 13). Again she bathes, almost ceremonially, and then she eats what appear to be two ritual meals. First she enters a room where she finds that though "no one was there . . . there was a cloth spread upon the table that stood against the wall, and a cover was laid for one, with a crusty brown loaf and a bottle of wine beside the plate." She bites "a piece from the brown loaf, tearing it with strong, white teeth" and drinks some of the wine. Then, after this solitary communion, she dines *à deux* with Robert, who serves her "no mean repast." Finally, as the sun sets, she and Robert sit—again ceremonially—at the feet of fat, matriarchal Madame Antoine, who tells them "legends of the Baratarians and the sea," so that as the moon rises Edna imagines she can hear "the whispering voices of dead men and the click of muffled gold" (chap. 13).

Having bathed, slept, feasted, communed, and received quasireligious instruction in an alternate theology, she seems definitively to have entered a fictive world, a realm of gold where extraordinary myths are real and ordinary reality is merely mythical. Yet of course the pagan fictive world Edna has entered is absolutely incompatible with the fictions of gentility and Christianity by which her "real" world lives. Metaphorically speaking, Edna has become Aphrodite, or at least an ephebe of that goddess. But what can be— must be—her fate? Shadowing her earlier "realism" with the subtextual romance she has developed in these chapters of swimming and boating, sleeping and eating, Chopin devotes the rest of her novel to examining with alternate sadness and sardonic verve the sequence of struggles for autonomy, understandings and misunderstandings, oppressions and exaltations, that she imagines would have befallen any nineteenth-century woman who experienced such a fantastic transformation. If Aphrodite—or at least Phaedra— were reborn as a *fin-de-siècle* New Orleans housewife, says Chopin, Edna Pontellier's fate would be her fate.

Because it is primarily a logical elaboration of the consequences of Edna's mythic metamorphosis, the rest of *The Awakening* can be summarized and analyzed quite briefly. Having awakened to her "true" self—that is, to a different and seemingly more authentic way of formulating her identity—Edna begins "daily casting aside that fictitious self which we assume like a garment with which to appear before the world." Yet as the self-consciously fictive episode on the Chênière Caminada reveals, neither she nor her author are eschewing fictions and fantasies altogether. Rather, Chopin has allowed the moon, the sea, the female summer colony, and Madame Antoine to re-create Edna Pontellier as a quasilegendary character in search of a story that can contain her and her power. That such a tale will be both hard to find and hard to tell, however, is revealed almost at once by Robert Le Brun's abrupt departure from Grand Isle. As the would-be lover of a newborn goddess, the Hippolytus to Edna's Phaedra, the Tristan to her Isolde, even the Léon to her Emma, he consciously struggles to do what is both morally and fictionally "right," accurately perceiving that because he is a "good" man and not a seducer, the traditional plot in which he imagines himself enmeshed now calls for renunciation. By the end of the novel, Edna will have created a different story, one in which Robert plays Adonis to her Venus, and, "no longer one of Mr. Pontellier's possessions to dispose of or not," she can declare that, like the Queen of Love, "I give myself where I choose" (chap. 36). But in chapter 15, as she struggles toward such an ambitious self-definition, she finds herself incapable of proposing any serious plot alternatives. Significantly, however, she does notice that Robert has announced his plans "in a high voice and with a lofty air [like] some gentlemen on the stage." Just as significantly, she retires to her cottage to tell her children a story that she does not, perhaps cannot, end, so that "instead of soothing, it excited them . . . [and] she left them in heated argument, speculating about the conclusion of the tale" (chap. 15).

The tale of her own life moves just as haltingly to its strange conclusion. As Edna becomes increasingly aware that she is "seeking herself and finding herself," she struggles with growing ferocity to discard and even destroy the conventions by which she has lived—her wedding ring, her "reception day," even her "charming home" that has been so well stocked with Mr. Pontellier's "household gods." Yet though she stamps on her ring, "striving to crush it . . . her small boot heel [does] not make an indenture, not a mark upon the little glittering circlet" (chap. 14). And though she plots to move out of her big house on Esplanade Street into a smaller cottage nearby, a home of her own she fictionalizes as the "Pigeon House," her husband counters with a fiction of his own "concerning the remodeling of his home, changes which he had long contemplated, and which he desired carried forward during his temporary absence" (chap. 32).

Edna's painting, her gambling, and her visits to the races as well as her relationships with Mlle. Reisz and Adèle Ratignolle, with the Flaubertian Alcée Arobin (clearly a sort of Rodolphe) and his friends Mr. and Mrs. Highcamp, constitute similar attempts at revisionary self-definition. Painting, for instance, allows her to recreate both her present and her past in more satisfactory forms. Mlle. Reisz brings her closer to Robert and to the oceanic passions and poetic ideas that had inspired her feelings for him from the first. Adèle Ratignolle reinforces her sense of the "blind contentment" implicit in the sequestered domesticity she has rejected (chap. 18). Her trips to the racetrack remind her of the freedom of her Kentucky childhood, when the "racehorse was a friend and intimate associate"—a spirit like herself, let loose in illimitable fields. And her rapidly developing sexual relationship with Arobin acts "like a narcotic upon her," offering her a "cup of life" that drugs and drains her awakening egotism even while her choice to drink it down manifests the new freedom she is attempting to define.

Yet none of these relationships succeed in yielding what we might call an open space in the plot that encloses Edna. In fact, precisely because these entanglements participate in a mutually agreed-upon social reality that gives them "realistic" plausibility as therapeutic possibilities, none is equal to the intensity of what is by now quite clearly Edna's metaphysical desire, the desire that has torn her away from her ordinary life into an extraordinary state where she has become, as Chopin's original title put it, "a solitary soul." Stranded in this state, having been visited by the Holy Ghost of the allegorical-sounding "Gulf," who rarely vouchsafes so much "ponderous" wisdom "to any woman," she can only struggle to make her own persuasive fictions, such as the story she tells at one point about "a woman who paddled away with her lover one night in a pirogue and never came back. They were lost amid the Baratarian Islands, and no one ever heard of them or found trace of them from that day to this" (chap. 23).

As Edna eventually realizes, however, even such a fiction defines desire through the banalities of second-rate romance, so that ultimately her dinner party in chapter 30 is the most authentic story she can tell and the one that is most radically revisionary. Here, as I began by noting, Edna Pontellier actually enacts the part of the person she has metaphorically become: "the regal woman, the one who rules, who looks on, who stands alone." Yet of course, in terms of the alternative theology that haunts Kate Chopin's story of this "solitary" heroine's mythologized life, the story of Edna's dinner party is the tale of a Last Supper, a final transformation of will and desire into bread and wine, flesh and blood, before the painful crucifixion of the "regal woman's" inevitable betrayal by a fictional scheme in which a regenerated Aphrodite has no viable role. More specifically, it is a Last Supper that precedes Edna's betrayal by a plot that sets both Adèle Ratignolle, the "mother-woman," and Robert Le Brun, the conventional lover, against her. In one way or another, each of these characters will remind her of her instrumentality—Adèle, exhausted by childbirth, whispering that she must "think of the children," and Robert passionately envisioning a transaction in which Mr. Pontellier might "set" her "free" to belong to *him*.

Finally, therefore, Edna can think of only one way "to elude them," to assert her autonomy, and to become absolutely herself, and that is through her much-debated suicidal last swim. Once again, however, our interpretation of this dénouement depends on our understanding of the mythic subtextual narrative that enriches it. Certainly if we see Edna's decision to swim into the sea's "abysses of solitude" as simply a "realistic" action, we are likely to disapprove of it, to consider it—as a number of critics have—"a defeat and a regression, rooted in a self-annihilating instinct, in a romantic incapacity to accommodate . . . to the limitations of reality." But though this may appear almost perversely metaphorical, I think it is possible to argue that Edna's last swim is not a suicide—that is, a death—at all, or, if it is a death, it is a death associated with a resurrection, a pagan, female Good Friday that promises a Venusian Easter. Certainly, at any rate, because of the way it is presented to us, Edna's supposed suicide enacts not a refusal to accommodate the limitations of reality but a subversive questioning of the limitations of both reality and "realism." For, swimming away from the white beach of Grand Isle, from the empty summer colony and the equally empty fictions of marriage and maternity, Edna swims, as the novel's last sentences tell us, not into death but back into her own life, back into her own vision, back into the imaginative openness of her childhood.

It is significant, after all, that in depicting Edna's last swim Chopin seems quite consciously to have swerved from precursors like Flaubert and Pierre Louÿs as well as from such a descendant as Edith Wharton, all of whom not only show the beautiful and desirous Aphroditean woman dead but actually linger over the details of her mortification. Flaubert, for instance, follows his sardonic Extreme Unction with horrifying visions of Emma's dead mouth "like a black hole at the bottom of her face," pouring forth "black liquid . . . as if she were vomiting." Similarly, in *Aphrodite* Pierre Louÿs undercuts his Chrysis's triumphant epiphany as Aphrodite with a ghastly picture of her dead body, a "thread of blood" flowing from one "diaphonous nostril" and ' some emerald-colored spots . . . softly [tinting] the relaxed belly." Even Wharton, in *The House of Mirth,* though she depicts the dead "semblance of Lily Bart" more gently, imagines her heroine's "estranged and tranquil face" definitively motionless and thereby, through that motionlessness, offering her watching lover "the word which made all clear." By contrast, Kate Chopin never allows Edna Pontellier to become fixed, immobilized. Neither perfected nor corrupted, she is still swimming when we last see her, nor does she ever in Dickinson's phrase, "Stop for Death." To be sure, we are told that "her arms and legs were growing tired," that "exhaustion was pressing upon and overpowering her" (chap. 39). It is clear enough that both reality and realism will contain her by fatiguing her, drowning her, killing her. Yet Chopin seems determined to regenerate Edna through a regeneration of romance, of fantasy.

No wonder, then, that as she enters the water for her last swim, this transformed heroine finally divests herself of "the unpleasant, pricking garments" of her old life as a "real" woman—a wife, mother, and mistress—and stands "naked under the sky . . . like some new-born creature, opening its eyes in a familiar world that it had never known." Together, her ceremonial nakedness, the paradoxically unknown familiarity of the world she is entering, and the "foamy wavelets [that curl and coil] like serpents about her ankles" (chap. 39) tell us that she is journeying not just toward rebirth but toward a regenerative and revisionary genre, a genre that intends to propose new realities for women by providing new mythic paradigms through which women's lives can be understood. Even in the last sentences of Chopin's novel, then, Edna Pontellier is still swimming. *And how, after all, do we know that she ever dies?* What critics have called her "suicide" is simply our interpretation of her motion, our realistic idea about the direction in which she is swimming. Yet as Chopin's last words tell us, that direction is toward the mythic, the pagan, the aphrodisiac. "There was the hum of bees, and the musky odor of pinks filled the air." Defeated, even crucified, by the "reality" of nineteenth-century New Orleans, Chopin's resurrected Venus is returning to Cyprus or Cythera.

This reading of *The Awakening* is of course hyperbolic, so that it is certainly not meant to displace those readings which honor the text's more obvious intentions. Rather, it is meant to suggest the argument between realistic and mythic aesthetic strategies that complicates and illuminates Chopin's brilliant novel. More, it is meant to make a few points about the literary history as well as the poetical significance of the goddess Aphrodite in the nineteenth and twentieth centuries. Finally, it is intended to clarify the dialectical relationship into which Chopin, as a pioneering feminist mythmaker, entered with such crucial precursors as Flaubert, Whitman, and Swinburne.

To take the last point first, I want to emphasize how important it is for us to remember that Chopin was a woman of the nineties, a writer of the *fin de siècle*. What did it mean, though, to be a *woman,* a female artist, of the *fin de siècle,* with all that such a faintly exotic, voluptuously apocalyptic French phrase implied? Superficially, at least, the *fin de siècle* meant, for literary women as for literary men, a kind of drawing room sophistication— smoking Turkish cigarettes, subscribing to *The Yellow Book,* reading (and translating) French fiction, all of which Kate Chopin did, especially in the St. Louis years of her widowhood, which were the years of her major literary activity. More centrally, the *fin de siècle* was associated, for women as for men, with artistic and intellectual revolutionaries like Beardsley and Wilde, together with their most significant precursors—Swinburne, Pater, Whitman, Wagner, Baudelaire. For women, however, the nineties also meant the comparatively new idea of "free love" as well as the even newer persona of "The New Woman." In addition, to be a woman of the nineties meant to have come of age in a new kind of literary era, one whose spirit was, if not dominated by literary women, at least shared and shaped by female imaginations. For it was only in the nineteenth century, after all, that women entered the profession of literature in significant numbers.

Such a sharing of the literary terrain had, however, double and mutually contradictory consequences. On the one hand, a number of male writers consciously or unconsciously perceived this commercial as well as aesthetic strengthening of the female imagination as a threatening cultural event. Belated heirs of a long patrilineage, they feared that with the entrance of women into high culture, history's originatory male center might no longer hold; lawless and unsponsored, the female imagination might fragment or even ruin civilization. On the other hand, women writers for the first time experienced the validation of a literary matrilineage. The earliest heiresses of a brief but notably enlivened cultural past, they now felt empowered to imagine a powerful future. At the same time, though, they had to contend against the male anxieties that saw them as the ruinous daughters of Herodias, rousing terrible winds of change and presaging apocalypse.

Given these cultural developments, it became inevitable that a work like *The Awakening* would enter into a complicated dialectic with contextual works by both male and female artists. If we once again compare Chopin's novel to its most obvious precursor, for instance—Flaubert's *Madame Bovary*—we can see that where the French writer dramatizes what he considers the destructive power of the female imagination, Chopin struggles to articulate what is positive in that power, never copying Flaubert (the way Cather and others thought she did) but always responding to him. Thus, for Flaubert, water is, as D. L. Demorest noted in 1931, "the symbol of Venus the delectable" (as it is for Chopin) but what this means in Flaubert's case is that throughout *Madame Bovary* "images of fluidity" dissolve and resolve to "evoke all that is disastrous in love." Emma's girlish sentimentality, for instance, is represented in what the writer himself called "milky oceans of books about castles and troubadours" while the final destructive horror of her imagination pours as black liquid, a sort of morbid ink, from her dead mouth, as if she were vomiting the essential fluid which had inscribed the romantic fictions that killed her and would eventually destroy her uxorious husband. Such Flaubertian images slowly filter the very idea of the fluid female imagination—the idea, that is, of female fluency—through what Sartre called "a realism more spiteful than detached" (and it is possible to speculate that they are general defensive strategies against the developing cultural power of women as well as specific defenses by which Flaubert armored himself against Louise Colet, a woman of letters on whom he felt helplessly dependent, defenses—to quote Sartre again—"in the diplomacy of Flaubert with regard to this pertinacious poetess"). Whatever the source of Flaubert's anxieties, however, Chopin vigorously defends herself and other literary women against such Flaubertian defenses, for she consistently revises his negative images of female "fluency" to present not a spitefully realistic but a metaphysically lyric version of the seductive mazes of the sea from which her Venus is born, substituting the valorizations of myth for the devaluations of realism.

But of course Chopin was aided in this revisionary struggle by aesthetic strategies learned from other precursors, both male and female. Surely, for example, she learned from Whitman and Swinburne, both of whom she much admired, to see the sea the way she did—as, implicitly, "a great sweet mother" uttering "the low and delicious word 'death'" even while rocking her heroine in life-giving "billowy drowse." In a sense, in fact, her Edna Pontellier is as much a cousin of the twenty-eight-year-old "twenty-ninth bather" in Whitman's *Song of Myself* as she is a niece of Flaubert's Emma Bovary. "Handsome and richly dressed," Edna, like Whitman's woman, has had "twenty-eight years of womanly life, and all so lonesome," hiding "aft the blinds of the window," and now, "dancing and laughing," she comes along the beach to bathe in the waters of life. Yet again, much as she had learned from Whitman, Chopin swerves from him, less radically than, but almost as significantly as, she had from Flaubert, to create a woman who does not enter the sea to "seize fast" to twenty-eight young men but rather to seize and hold fast to herself. Similarly, she swerves from Swinburne to create an ocean that is not simply an other—a "fair, green-girdled mother"—

but also a version of *self*, intricately veined with "mazes of inward contemplation" and sacramental precisely because emblematic of such subjectivity.

In this last respect, indeed, the sea of Chopin's *Awakening* has much in common with the mystically voluptuous ocean Emily Dickinson imagines in a love poem like "Wild Nights—Wild Nights!" For when Dickinson exclaims "Rowing in Eden— / Ah, the Sea! / Might I but moor—Tonight— / In Thee!," she is imagining an ocean of erotic energy that will transform and transport her, an ocean that exists *for* her and in some sense *is* her. More, in identifying this sea with Eden, she is revising the vocabulary of traditional Christian theology so as to force it to reflect the autonomy and urgency of female desire. Such a revision is of course exactly the one that Chopin performed throughout *The Awakening*. Thus where the Extreme Unction that Flaubert intones over the corpse of Emma Bovary (stroking the oil of reductive metaphor over her no longer impassioned eyes, nostrils, lips, hands, and feet) functions as a final, misogynistic exorcism of the ferocity of the imagining and desirous woman, Kate Chopin's redefined sacraments of bread and wine or crimson cocktails function, like Dickinson's, to vindicate female desire in yet another way. For in creating a heroine as free and golden as Aphrodite, a "regal woman" who "stands alone" and gives herself where she "pleases," Chopin was exploring a vein of revisionary mythology allied not only to the revisionary erotics of free love advocates like Victoria Woodhull and Emma Goldmann but also to the feminist theology of women like Florence Nightingale, who believed that the next Christ might be a "female Christ," and Mary Baker Eddy, who argued that because "the ideal woman corresponds to life and to Love . . . we have not as much authority for considering God masculine as we have for considering Him feminine, for Love imparts the clearest idea of Deity." Finally, therefore, Chopin's allusive subtextual narrative of the second coming of Aphrodite becomes an important step in the historical female struggle to imagine a deity who would rule and represent a strong female community, a woman's colony transformed into a woman's country.

To be sure, men from Wagner (in *Tannhäuser*) to Baudelaire (writing on Wagner), Swinburne (in "Lais Veneris," "Sapphics," and, by implication, his version of "Phaedra"), Beardsley (in "Under the Hill"), and Pierre Louÿs (in *Aphrodite* and *Songs of Bilitis*) had begun to examine the characteristics of the goddess of love, who had in the past, as Paul Friedrich points out in his useful study of *The Meaning of Aphrodite,* often been "avoided" by poets and scholars because they found her female erotic autonomy both "alarming" and "alluring." But for the most part even these revolutionary nineteenth-century artists used Aphrodite the way Flaubert used Emma Bovary—to enact a new anxiety about female power. For Chopin, however, as for such feminist descendants as Isadora Duncan and H. D., Aphrodite/Venus becomes a radiant symbol of the erotic liberation that turn-of-the-century women had begun to allow themselves to desire.

The source of Aphrodite's significance for this revisionary company of women is not hard to discern. Neither primarily wife (like Hera), mother (like Demeter), nor daughter (like Athena), Aphrodite is, and has her sexual energy, for herself, her own grandeur, her own pleasure. As Friedrich observes, moreover, all her essential characteristics—her connections with birds and water, her affinity for young mortal men, her nakedness, her goldenness, and even her liminality, as well as her erotic sophistication—empower her in one way or another. Her dove- or swan-drawn chariot enables her to travel between earth and sky, while her sea-birth places her between earth and sea. Naked yet immortal, she moves with ease and grace between the natural and the supernatural, the human and the inhuman, nature and culture. Golden and decked in gold, she is associated with sunset and sunrise, the liminal hours of transformative consciousness—the entranced hours of awakening or drowsing—that mediate between night and day, dream and reality. Almost inevitably, then, she is the patron goddess of Sappho, whom that paradigmatic literary feminist Virginia Woolf called "the supreme head of song" and whose lyric imagination famously fostered and was fostered by unique erotic freedom. Inevitably, too, she became a crucial image of female divinity in the increasingly feminist years of the *fin de siècle,* and almost as inevitably Kate Chopin (perhaps half-consciously, perhaps consciously) made her a model for a "regal" sea-borne, gold-clad, bird-haunted woman whose autonomous desire for freedom, and for a younger man, edged her first out of a large patriarchal mansion into a small female cottage and then across the shadowline that separates the clothing of culture from the nakedness of nature.

It is no coincidence, after all, that Kate Chopin imagined her Venus rising from the foam of a ceremonial dinner party in 1899, the same year that another American artist, Isadora Duncan, was beginning to dance the dances of Aphrodite in London salons while the feminist classicist Jane Ellen Harrison, who would soon recover the matriarchal origins of ancient Greek religion, chanted Greek lyrics in the background. Within a few years, Duncan, haunted by her own birth "under the star of Aphrodite," was to sit "for days before the *Primavera,* the famous painting of Botticelli" and create a dance "in which I endeavoured to realise the soft and marvelous movements emanating from it; the circle of nymphs and the flight of the Zephyrs, all assembling about the central figure, half Aphrodite, half Madonna, who indicates the procreation of spring in one significant gesture." Musing on the "sweet, half-seen pagan life, where Aphrodite gleamed through the form of the gracious but more tender Mother of Christ," this prophetess of the beauty of female nakedness was struggling, as Chopin had, to see the power of the pagan through the constraints of the Christian and the triumph of the female through the power of the pagan. She was striving, as H. D. would, to "relight the flame" of "Aphrodite, holy name," and of "Venus, whose name is kin / to venerate, / venerator." And she was laboring, as Chopin had, to define the indefinable mythic essence of "a familiar world that [she] had never known."

Like Chopin's and H. D.'s, too, Duncan's revisionary program marked an apex of feminist confidence in the female erotic autonomy of Aphrodite. But even as these artists struggled to reimagine and reappropriate the ancient powers of the Queen of Love, a few literary women who were their contemporaries or descendants had begun to formulate darker counterimaginings, visions of Venus in which the old feminine mistrust of female sensuality surfaced once again. Most notable among these visions is Willa Cather's sardonically brilliant "Coming, Aphrodite!," a retelling of Louÿs's *Aphrodite* which seems also to revise and subvert the allusive terms of *The Awakening*, and to do this so dramatically that it might almost be considered an extension of Cather's earlier censorious review of Chopin's book. Specifically, Cather's story presents us with an ambitious Illinois farm girl named *Edna* Bowers who, along with devouring "Sapho" [sic] and "Mademoiselle de Maupin," has resolved to become a great actress-singer named "Eden Bower." Just as important, she has easily and casually stepped outside of ordinary social confinement and made herself erotically autonomous. When the story begins, she is being kept (entirely for her own convenience and in the furtherance of her career) by a handily absent Chicago millionaire in a New York flat next door to a studio occupied by Don Hedger, a struggling artist. Tracing the stages of their romance, Cather splits Chopin's erotic and artistic Edna into two characters: the metaphysically awakened painter, who falls in love with Eden by peering at her through a hole in the wall of his closet, and the physically awakened Eden, whom he watches as, like a latterday Isadora, she exercises naked before a mirror until, like both Edna and Isadora, she takes on a mythic radiance. Thus, at the tale's most intense, Hedger thinks of her body "as never having been clad, or as having worn the stuffs and dyes of all the centuries but his own. And for him [Eden has] no geographical associations; unless with Crete, or Alexandria, or Veronese's Venice. She [is] the immortal conception, the perennial theme."

Throughout the tale, however, Cather hints that when this naked Aphrodite ceases to be paradigmatic and becomes personal, or to put it differently, when she refuses to be merely an artwork—a "conception" or a "theme"—and asserts herself as an autonomous being, she becomes not an embodiment of Eden but a troublesome and anti-Edenic Eve. Early on, for instance, she threatens Hedger's masculinity by scorning his phallic bulldog, Caesar (who does, in fact, "seize her" and is in return seized and silenced by his master, who has himself been seized and stupefied by desire). Later, when Hedger tells an extravagant story about a sexually voracious Aztec princess who gelds and enslaves a captive prince, we understand the fable to be a monitory one: the power of female desire may be castrating, even murderous. Finally, therefore, Cather separates the lovers with the suggestion that Eden's sensual desirousness also implies a material greed that would ruin the aesthetic career of Hedger, the "true" artist. And indeed, by the end of the tale this anti-Edenic Eve's autonomy and ambition have led to a death of the soul even more terrible than the dissolution Cather associated with Edna Pontellier's erotic dreams. Now a major international star, scheduled to sing in an operatic version of Louÿs's *Aphrodite,* Eden has learned that Hedger, whom she hasn't seen in twenty years, has become an originary figure, "decidedly an influence in art," and it is plain that he has become this by freeing himself from her influence. As she drives off in her luxurious car her face becomes "hard and settled, like a plaster cast; so a sail, that has been filled by a strong breeze, behaves when the wind suddenly dies. Tomorrow night the wind would blow again, and this mask would be the golden face of Aphrodite. But a 'big' career takes its toll, even with the best of luck." Cather's point seems clear: as in Louÿs's novel and as in Hedger's fable of "The Forty Lovers of the Queen," female erotic autonomy, imaged in the golden nakedness of Aphrodite, is inexorably doomed to rigidify and reify, killing not only any lover unlucky enough to remain captive but also the shining queen of love herself.

There is no doubt, of course, that Willa Cather had a number of personal motives for writing a story like "Coming, Aphrodite!" which reimagines Aphrodite so bitterly. These motives probably included both a deep anxiety about heterosexual desire and a deep identification with the closeted artist who admires and desires the naked girl next door. When we look at the tale as a revisionary critique of *The Awakening,* however, we can see that the creator of Edna/Eden Bower(s) is withdrawing unsympathetically from Chopin's Edna precisely because the earlier Aphrodite had to swim away from the solid ground of patriarchal reality and die into what was no more than a myth of erotic power. As Mlle. Reisz tells Edna, the artist "must possess the courageous soul. . . . The brave soul. The soul that dares and defies" (chap. 21), but Edna, naked and defeated on the beach, is haunted by a bird with a broken wing, "reeling, fluttering, circling disabled down, down to the water" (chap. 38). Given her own anxieties, Cather must have needed to clarify this problem for herself; and after all, her anxieties about female eroticism were representatively female even while they had personal origins; more, they were anxieties that accurately (if paradoxically) summarized Chopin's own wounded reaction to the hostile reviews *The Awakening* received from, among others, Willa Cather. Thus, Cather implicitly decides in "Coming, Aphrodite!" that Edna Pontellier cannot be an artist because she is desirous; art, which requires courage and demands survival, must be left to the (male) Hedgers of this world, who hedge their bets by renouncing desire and protecting themselves against women with a snarling canine Caesar. Yet as Chopin keenly understood, it is precisely because she is desirous that Edna becomes an artist in the first place, and her art, as at her dinner party, is as much an art of eroticism as it is a "pure" aesthetic activity.

What is the way out of this vicious circle? Even so recent a descendant of Chopin, Cather, Duncan, and H. D. as Anne Sexton could see none. In a posthumous volume, *Words for Dr. Y.,* her daughter Linda Gray Sexton prints a piece called "To Like, To Love" in which the poet addresses "Aphrodite, / my Cape Town lady, / my mother, my daughter" and admits that though "I dream you Nordic and six foot tall, / I dream you masked and blood-mouthed," in the end "you start to cry, / you fall down into a huddle, / you are sick . . . because you are no one." It is as if for women, struggling to recapture the autonomy of desire, there was one moment of Aphroditean rebirth—the neo-Swinburnian moment, say, when Edna enthroned herself in gold satin at the head of a fictive dinner table and Isadora Duncan theatrically brooded before Botticelli's *Primavera*—and then, as Virginia Woolf wrote of the erotic in a slightly different context, "the close withdrew; the hard softened. It was over—the moment." "Realism," declares Cather, may be more than a fictional mode; it may in fact reflect a social reality in which the golden Aphrodite is no more than a metal mask.

Perhaps it is not insignificant, then, that among recent poets it is a male artist, Wallace Stevens, who would have responded most sympathetically to the desire implicit in the allusive structure of the tale Kate Chopin's *The Awakening* tells, for he would have been free from the anxieties that serious identification with a mythic figure necessarily entails, free as Swinburne, for instance, was, and as neither Chopin nor Cather could ever be. Certainly when Stevens's "paltry nude" starts, like Edna Pontellier, on her early voyage, he too imagines a second coming, not of a rough beast like the slouching nightmare creature of Yeats's visionary apocalypse, but of a "goldener nude," a more triumphantly secular goddess, "of a later day." Still, because Chopin was a woman writer, her imagining was at least as different from his as his was from Yeats's. She, after all, painfully dreamed a surrogate self into that visionary nakedness. Imagining (even if failing to achieve) transformation, she was haunted by her longing for a redeemed and redemptive Aphrodite, who would go "like the centre of sea-green pomp" into a future of different myths and mythic difference.

KATHLEEN MARGARET LANT

The Siren of Grand Isle:
Adèle's Role in The Awakening

Most critics of Kate Chopin's *The Awakening* (1899) emphasize the role of Léonce Pontellier, Robert Lebrun, and Alcée Arobin in Edna's awakening. Per Seyersted says, for example, that "It is of course Edna's three men who serve as the real catalysts for her double awakening" to both her intellectual and sensuous nature. Kenneth Eble insists that Robert alone first moves Edna: "Robert Lebrun is the young man who first awakens, or rather, is present at the awakening of Edna Pontellier into passion." Such assertions proceed from a male-centered approach to the work, which does not allow that Edna, as a woman, could be stirred by other than a man, and from a failure to read the novel as Chopin has written it.

Chopin makes it clear, in fact, that Edna's first awakening is to Adèle Ratignolle, who vacations on Grand Isle with her; characterizing Edna's reasons for initiating her quest for self-discovery, Chopin observes,

> There may have been—there must have been—influences, both subtle and apparent, working in their several ways to induce her to do this; but the most obvious was the influence of Adèle Ratignolle.

In Adèle, Chopin has created a siren figure who both lures and imperils Edna, a human counterpart to the seductive sea that beckons to Edna's soul, inviting her to swim. Adèle is not simply emotionally appealing to Edna; she

---

From *Southern Studies: An Interdisciplinary Journal of the South* 23, no. 2 (Summer 1984). © 1984 by the Southern Studies Institute.

is also physically attractive, and here on her island in the sea she invites Edna to embark upon the ultimately solitary journey that eventually destroys her. It is with Adèle that Edna begins her awakening, hopefully, and it is with Adèle, too, that Edna's awakening ends, with disillusionment and utter despair. In her initial response to Adèle, Edna awakens to two facets of her own character: her artistic temperament and responsiveness to beauty and her own feminine sensuousness, which she finds reflected alluringly in Adèle:

> The excessive physical charm of the Creole had first attracted her, for Edna had a sensuous susceptibility to beauty. Then the candor of the woman's whole existence, which every one might read, and which formed so striking a contrast to her own habitual reserve— this might have furnished a link. Who can tell what metals the gods use in forging the subtle bond which we call sympathy, which we might as well call love.

Adèle and the sea, then, two powerful avatars of the eternally feminine, initiate Edna's exploration of her relationship with the universe. The first six chapters of Chopin's novel set Edna's divided personality before us; Edna has discovered that she lives two lives—the "inward life which questions," which wonders, which dreams and the "outward existence which conforms," which stifles and oppresses her. In chapter 7 Edna begins, with Adèle as her muse and guide, to explore the inner life, which she has never experienced fully. With Adèle, Edna is stimulated to look within and to question seriously. By the end of the chapter, Edna has begun her quest:

> Edna did not reveal so much as all this to Madame Ratignolle that summer day when they sat with faces turned to the sea. But a good part of it escaped her. She had put her head down on Madame Ratignolle's shoulder. She was flushed and felt intoxicated with the sound of her own voice and the unaccustomed taste of candor. It muddled her like wine, or like a first breath of freedom.

In order for Adèle's being to work its liberating magic upon Edna, the two women must escape the forces—men and children—which, Chopin demonstrates, come eternally between a woman and her own desires. As a true representative of femininity, Adèle is excessively devoted to her husband and to her children, that is, to her womanly role; and Edna, as a sensual human being, finds herself powerfully drawn to Robert. Nevertheless, the complete immersion of Edna in the self requires her total involvement with the feminine, with Adèle. Only by leaving non-feminine others behind can Edna explore her self. Adèle and Edna's walk to the beach is conveyed in terms of both renunciation and escape:

> The two women went away one morning to the beach together, arm in arm, under the huge white sunshade. Edna had prevailed upon Madame Ratignolle to leave the children behind, though she could not induce her to relinquish a diminutive roll of needlework, which Adèle begged to be allowed to slip into the depths of her pocket. In some unaccountable way they had escaped from Robert.

The charm and freedom for Edna in being with Adèle is, then, a direct function of Adèle's femininity; her figure is "feminine and matronly," and her style of dress is frivolous and womanly: "She was dressed in pure white, with a fluffiness of ruffles that became her." Both Edna and Adèle, selecting an appropriate place to seat themselves, commence an elaborate unveiling and readjusting of garments, which prefigure the emotional unveiling and reevaluation to come:

> Madame Ratignolle removed her veil, wiped her face with a rather delicate handkerchief, and fanned herself with the fan which she always carried suspended about her person by a long narrow ribbon. Edna removed her collar and opened her dress at the throat. . . . there was a breeze blowing, a choppy, stiff wind that whipped the water into froth. It fluttered the skirts of the two women and kept them for a while engaged in adjusting, readjusting, tucking in, securing hair-pins and hat-pins.

In a similar manner Edna begins to readjust her responses to life. Adèle asks Edna what she is thinking, and Edna's first response is concealment, an effort to maintain the protective division she has created between her precious inner life and her functional persona. In her first attempt to be honest, however, Edna reconsiders her answer:

> "Of whom—of what are you thinking?" asked Adèle. . . .
> "Nothing," returned Mrs. Pontellier, with a start, adding at once: "How stupid! But it seems to me it is the reply we make instinctively to such a question. Let me see," she went on, throwing back her head and narrowing her fine eyes until they shone like two vivid points of light. "Let me see. I was really not conscious of thinking of anything; but perhaps I can retrace my thoughts."

By means of a kind of free association, Edna begins to examine her own thought processes, although Adèle declares that it is far too hot to think, "especially to think about thinking."

Edna persists, and discovers that her thoughts carry her back to a day in childhood when she was "running away from prayers," running away from the family and her father and the "gloom" of her duties. Adèle again lures Edna on, asking the appropriate question, "And have you been running away from prayers ever since, *ma chère?*" Edna is quick to answer that she has not, but she tells Adèle that her thoughts and her life have recently taken on the freedom and rebelliousness that characterized her childhood flights:

> "But do you know," she broke off, turning her quick eyes upon Madame Ratignolle and leaning forward a little so as to bring her face quite close to that of her companion, "sometimes I feel this summer as if I were walking through the green meadow again; idly, aimlessly, unthinking and unguided."

Edna says that crossing that meadow as a child, she "threw out her arms as if swimming when she walked, beating the tall grass as one strikes out in the water." Now, as an adult, she must learn to swim in another sea if she is to traverse safely the sea of her own personality, the ocean of her unguided, undirected experience of life as a woman.

Sitting on the beach with Adèle, Edna's thoughts range over her other relations to the universe as well. She remembers adolescent infatuations with a cavalry officer, with a young gentleman, and—this one more serious—with a tragedian. She considers her relationship to her husband, Léonce, of whom she is fond, but who can never awaken in her the "romance and dreams" of her love for the actor. With respect to her marriage, "Edna found herself face to face with the realities"; she enjoys a kind of security in the flaccidity of her relationship with Léonce:

> She grew fond of her husband, realizing with some unaccountable satisfaction that no trace of passion or excessive and fictitious warmth colored her affection, thereby threatening its dissolution.

Her love for her children is colored by the same desire for freedom. Edna is "fond of her children in an uneven, impulsive way," but she feels liberated, more herself, when they are gone:

> Their absence was a sort of relief, though she did not admit this, even to herself. It seemed to free her of a responsibility which she had blindly assumed and for which Fate had not fitted her.

Edna's incipient, faltering attempts to explore her own character and to obliterate the barrier between her secret self and her publicly acceptable persona come to an end when she and Adèle are driven from their feminine solitude by the sound of voices: "It was Robert, surrounded by a troop of children, searching for them." Men and children, for Edna the two great impediments to a union with the self, have reclaimed the two women.

Edna's goal is twofold after her introspective time with Adèle. She becomes aware, in the first place, of her need for freedom; she desires the liberty to choose, to follow her own soul's direction. In the second place, she wishes to be aware of these dictates of her soul, to make choices based upon what she discovers to be her own needs. She wants both the freedom of thought to know herself and the freedom of choice to act upon her knowledge. What she discovers is that although several possibilities exist for her, they exist exclusively; by choosing one, she forsakes the others. She finds many selves from which to select, but she sees ultimately that they are just that—selves, entities which mask, obscure, or obliterate her own inner life.

Although Adèle by her physical beauty initiates Edna's awakening to her own physical needs, Adèle does not provide for Edna a model for a suitable self. Edna can admire Adèle's charm and can be stimulated and moved by it, but Edna cannot be Adèle. For Edna, the female life of sensuousness and physical fulfillment is constricting. Adèle is a "mother-woman"; she lives to produce and care for children. This role, Chopin observes, suits many women at Grand Isle admirably:

> The mother-women seemed to prevail that summer at Grand Isle.
> It was easy to know them, fluttering about with extended, protecting wings when any harms, real or imaginary, threatened their precious brood. They were women who idolized their children, worshiped their husbands, and esteemed it a holy privilege to efface themselves as individuals and grow wings as ministering angels.

For such a self-effacing role, Edna declares herself eminently unsuited. Edna is a woman of a new sort, but Adèle is a woman of a passing world and an ancient order: "There are no words to describe her save the old ones that have served so often to picture the bygone heroine of romance and the fair lady of our dreams." While Adèle in her femininity serves as a catalyst to Edna's growing self-awareness, she is herself trite and obvious ("There was nothing subtle or hidden about her charms"), even overdone and contrived ("She was growing a little stout, but it did not seem to detract an iota from the grace of every step, pose, gesture").

In fact, the impossibility for Edna of choosing a life like Adèle's becomes clear when Edna and Adèle have "a rather heated argument" over Adèle's excessive preoccupation with the accepted feminine role of wife and mother. While Edna loves her sons, she does not devote herself exclusively to them; she tells Adèle bluntly, "I would give my life for my children; but I wouldn't give myself." As at other turning points in *The Awakening,* Edna discovers that most people do not begin to fathom what she means: "the two women did not appear to understand each other or to be talking the same language." Edna is engaged in the process of discovering her self; such a process involves discarding false concepts of who she is and what she can do. Of her feeling for her children and her role as wife and mother, she tells Adèle, "it's only something which I am beginning to comprehend, which is revealing itself to me." That Adèle has simply assumed a role that conventional morality has designated as hers is revealed by her rejoinder, a rejoinder which demonstrates her complete failure to grasp Edna's point: "a woman who would give her life for her children could no more than that—your Bible tells you so."

If Edna cannot give up the sense of self that Adèle ignorantly relinquishes, she cannot, on the other hand, renounce the sexuality and sensuousness of her own nature that she finds reflected appealingly in Adèle. For this reason, she cannot choose a life like Mademoiselle Reisz's, devoted solely to art. Mademoiselle Reisz, a pianist, is unmarried, despises children, and behaves rudely to everyone. When she is to play for those assembled for an evening at Grand Isle, the children are sent to bed; she objects, moreover, to the "crying of a baby." Mademoiselle Reisz is a woman completely alone, devoted only to herself:

> She was a disagreeable little woman, no longer young, who had quarreled with almost every one, owing to a temper which was self-assertive and a disposition to trample on the rights of others.

Mademoiselle Reisz recognizes the artist in Edna, who paints and sketches, and tells Edna, "You are the only one worth playing for." Later she advises Edna to devote herself to her art, to be strong and to believe in herself: "to succeed, the artist must possess the courageous soul. . . . The brave soul. The soul that dares and defies." Edna does have the soul that dares and defies, but ultimately Mademoiselle Reisz and the artist's life prove as inappropriate a choice for Edna as the more acceptable domestic life of Adèle.

While Adèle's sensuousness awakens Edna's sense of self, Adèle is without a self; she gives it up to become a "mother-woman." Conversely, Mademoiselle Reisz's piano playing, for her an exercise of will, awakens Edna's sensuousness; as Edna listens

> the very passions themselves were aroused within her soul, sway-
> ing it, lashing it, as the waves daily beat upon her splendid body.
> She trembled, she was choking, and the tears blinded her.

Mademoiselle Reisz is herself without passion. She does not swim, does not immerse herself in experience, and she is without appetite and desire: "She habitually ate chocolates for their sustaining quality; they contained much nutriment in small compass, she said." Adèle, the wife and mother, is without a self; Mademoiselle Reisz, the celibate artist, is without passion. Like the two nameless lovers and the obsessively religious old woman in black, who walk silently through the pages of the novel, Adèle and Mademoiselle Reisz represent the extremes of personality, which for Edna are impossible. To choose one of these extremes of personality as a model is, for Edna, to negate part of herself. Edna's awareness of her predicament sharpens because of her initial attraction to and involvement with Adèle. It is Adèle who first awakens Edna.

The three men in Edna's life, whom most critics of the novel find re- sponsible for her awakening, serve—as Adèle and Mademoiselle Reisz do— as representatives of various possible selves available to Edna. Her husband, Léonce, demands the same Edna that Edna perceives—and rejects—in Adèle. Léonce wants a "mother woman." Robert Lebrun and Alcée Arobin offer two other possible selves for Edna, which prove finally unacceptable. To choose one involves a rejection of some part of herself that Edna cannot give up. Robert stirs Edna's romantic longing. He offers attention, flattery, and protestations of undying devotion. At every point, his sincerity is impugned (Adèle tells him to be careful or Edna will make the mistake of taking him seriously; Chopin hints that he has been involved with a woman in Mexico and with Mariequita on Grand Isle), but Edna believes in him and falls in love with him.

Their attachment is eminently adolescent, filled with escapes to en- chanted islands, tearful letters, longing, yearning, and dreary separations. Robert seems more capable of recognizing the immaturity of their liaison than Edna, for he is content to maintain the flirtation, but he does not wish to consummate the relationship. When Edna seems perilously close to de- claring her physical desire for Robert as she has declared her love, he retreats as quickly as possible, leaving a chivalrous and cold note in farewell: "I love you. Good-by—because I love you."

The shallowness of Robert's affection becomes obvious in the cowardice of his dealings with Edna. As a flirtatious, romantic intrigue she does not threaten him, but as a sexually demanding woman, she is formidable, more than he can cope with. Many critics of *The Awakening* attribute Edna's eventual suicide to her disappointment at Robert's leaving her. She is hurt, but not destroyed. Robert has offered yet another role to Edna, another self— woman in love. That this self is as partial as the others, she reveals before her suicide. She loves Robert, but not even he proves irreplaceable, essential to her being:

> There was no human being whom she wanted near her except
> Robert and she even realized that the day would come when he,
> too, and the thought of him would melt out of her existence,
> leaving her alone.

If Robert offers love and romantic illusion without physical passion, Alcée Arobin, the devastatingly attractive libertine, offers sexuality without affection. He stirs a part of Edna that has slumbered through her marriage as well as through her romantic infatuation with Robert:

> His eyes were very near. He leaned upon the lounge with an arm
> extended across her, while the other hand still rested on her hair.
> They continued silently to look into each other's eyes. When he
> leaned forward and kissed her, she clasped his head, holding his
> lips to hers.
> It was the first kiss of her life to which her nature had really
> responded. It was a flaming torch that kindled desire.

But Arobin, too, reaches only a part of Edna; awake to her body, she forsakes the love her soul craves. She knows he is but the first of a series of affairs:

> She had said over and over to herself: "To-day it is Arobin; to-
> morrow it will be some one else. It makes no difference to me."

At this point, Edna's predicament is not uniquely feminine. What she experiences is a universal human longing to divest the authentic self of the false selves that stifle it. None of the selves available to Edna is enough; each involves a renunciation of another part of Edna vital to her existence. Edna's greatest freedom comes in her ability to give these false selves up, to desist from her characteristically feminine way of coping with them—by means of hiding the real and revealing the false selves—and to live, if necessary, in solitude. She can at least preserve her integrity by means of renunciation. Independently, she can swim "where no woman had swum before"; she can swim away from the shore, the people, the limitations of life into the sea, into the female, the "unlimited." Her initial awakening to the feminine in Adèle could end with a triumphant mingling of her self with the feminine, with the sea. And many readers of *The Awakening* do find Edna's death a triumphant transcendence of the limitations of the roles imposed upon her.

There is one role, one requirement, she cannot relinquish, and that is biological motherhood. Edna can reject the social role of "mother-woman," but she can never escape her biological connection to her sons; they are always with her, demanding:

> The children appeared before her like antagonists who had over-come her; who had overpowered and sought to drag her into the soul's slavery for the rest of her days.

Appropriately, Adèle Ratignolle, who siren-like first enticed Edna to her journey in the sea, is the agent responsible for her destruction in the sea. Called to Adèle's confinement, Edna witnesses the birth of Adèle's child, and she recalls her own lying-in with fear and horror. Giving birth is the ultimate sleep, the final giving up of will:

> Edna began to feel uneasy. She was seized with a vague dread. Her own like experiences seemed far away, unreal, and only half remembered. She recalled faintly an ecstacy of pain, the heavy odor of chloroform, a stupor which had deadened sensation.

Against the biological necessity that must "secure mothers for the race" and against the biological imperative a woman feels to care for her children (Adèle reminds Edna of this when she says, "Think of the children, Edna. Oh think of the children! Remember them!"), Edna rebels. She will not be made use of, owned "body and soul"; she will reserve the right to renounce any self or role unsuitable to her. At Adèle's side, she attempts to reject the biological exploitation of motherhood:

> With an inward agony, with a flaming, outspoken revolt against the ways of Nature, she witnessed the scene of torture.

Finally, however, Edna realizes that there is one self she cannot refuse, for this self is a product of her physical being; the only way to renounce biology is to renounce the physical self. She has given up the dual life of secrecy, conformity, and lies, which concealed her questions and assertiveness. She has tossed off the garments of false selves; she has learned to swim, to master the waves and move away from the shore to freedom. But she cannot renounce her sons; she can only "elude them," and she must give up the body to elude her sons. In so doing she must lose the self; she must *not* swim. Her situation is hopeless. She has awakened because the feminine Adèle has stirred her to explore her own feminine inner landscape. But tragically, again because Adèle exposes her to the ultimate reality of femininity, Edna awakens to the horrible knowledge that she can never, because she is female, be her own person.

Chronology

1851   Kate O'Flaherty born in St. Louis, Missouri, on February 8.

1855   Kate's father dies in a train wreck.

1868   Graduates from the St. Louis Academy of the Sacred Heart. Moves to New Orleans.

1870   Kate marries a Creole, Oscar Chopin, in New Orleans.

1879   The Chopins move to a cotton plantation near Cloutierville, Natchitoches Parish, in north central Louisiana.

1882   Oscar Chopin succumbs to swamp fever.

1883   Kate, unable to work the plantation alone, returns to her mother's home in St. Louis with her six children.

1885   Chopin's mother dies.

1888   Chopin's first published work, "If it might be," a poem, appears in *America*, a progressive Chicago magazine. Begins work on "Euphrasie," published later as "A No Account Creole."

1889   Chopin publishes two stories, "Wiser than a God" and "A Point at Issue!" Begins to write *At Fault*.

1890   *At Fault* published.

1891   "Young Dr. Gosse" written, sent to several publishers, but never accepted.

1894   Houghton Mifflin publishes *Bayou Folk*, twenty-three short stories written between 1891 and 1894. Chopin's stories appear in *Century, Atlantic,* and *Vogue*.

1896   Chopin, frustrated by the repeated rejection of "Young Dr. Gosse,"
        destroys the manuscript.

1897   *A Night in Acadie,* containing twenty-one stories, published. Cho-
        pin begins work on *The Awakening.*

1898   "The Storm" written.

1899   *The Awakening* published.

1900   Short story "Charlie" written, but not published until after Cho-
        pin's death.

1904   On a visit to the St. Louis World's Fair, Chopin suffers a cerebral
        hemorrhage and dies two days later, on August 22.

Contributors

HAROLD BLOOM, Sterling Professor of the Humanities at Yale University, is the author of *The Anxiety of Influence, Poetry and Repression,* and many other volumes of literary criticism. His forthcoming study, *Freud: Transference and Authority,* attempts a full-scale reading of all of Freud's major writings. A MacArthur Prize Fellow, he is general editor of five series of literary criticism published by Chelsea House.

KENNETH EBLE teaches English at the University of Utah. His books include studies of F. Scott Fitzgerald, Mark Twain, and William Dean Howells.

LARZER ZIFF is Caroline Donovan Professor of English at The Johns Hopkins University. His books include *Puritanism in America, The American 1890s,* and *Literary Democracy.*

DONALD A. RINGE teaches English at the University of Kentucky. He is the author of *American Gothic: Imagination and Reason in Nineteenth-Century Fiction* and *The Pictorial Mode: Space and Time in the Art of Bryant, Irving, and Cooper.*

CYNTHIA GRIFFIN WOLFF is Professor of English and American Literature at MIT. She is the editor of *Classic American Women Writers,* and the author of *Samuel Richardson and the Eighteenth-Century Puritan Character* and *A Feast of Words: The Triumph of Edith Wharton.*

SUSAN J. ROSOWSKI teaches English at the University of Nebraska.

JOYCE C. DYER teaches English at the Western Reserve Academy in Hudson, Ohio.

ELAINE GARDINER is Assistant Professor of English at Washburn University.

SANDRA M. GILBERT, Professor of English at Princeton University, is the author, with Susan Gubar, of *The Madwoman in the Attic: The Woman Writer and the Nineteenth-Century Literary Imagination*. She is also editor, with Ms. Gubar, of *The Norton Anthology of Women's Literature* and *Shakespeare's Sisters: Feminist Essays on Women Poets*.

KATHLEEN MARGARET LANT is Assistant Professor of English at California Polytechnic State University.

Bibliography

Arms, George. "Kate Chopin's *The Awakening* in the Perspective of Her Literary Career." In *Essays on American Literature in Honor of Jay B. Hubbell,* edited by Clarence Gohdes. Durham, N.C.: Duke University Press, 1967.

Arner, Robert. "Kate Chopin." *Louisiana Studies* 14 (Spring 1975): 111–39.

Bonner, Thomas. "Christianity and Catholicism in the Fiction of Kate Chopin." *The Southern Quarterly* 20, no. 2 (Winter 1982): 118–25.

———. "Kate Chopin's *At Fault* and *The Awakening:* A Study in Structure." *Markham Review* 7 (1977): 10–14.

Burchard, Gina M. "Kate Chopin's Problematical Womanliness: The Frontier of American Feminism." *Journal of the American Studies Association of Texas* 15 (1984): 35–45.

Cantwell, Robert. "*The Awakening* by Kate Chopin." *The Georgia Review* 10 (Winter 1956): 489–94.

Casale, Ottavio Mark. "Beyond Sex: The Dark Romanticism of Kate Chopin's *The Awakening.*" *Ball State University Forum* 19 (1978): 76–80.

Dyer, Joyce C. "The Restive Brute: The Symbolic Presentation of Repression and Sublimation in Kate Chopin's 'Fedora.'" *Studies in Short Fiction* 18, no. 3 (Summer 1981): 261–66.

Forrey, Carolyn. "The New Woman Revisited." *Women's Studies* 2 (1974): 37–56.

Justus, James H. "The Unwakening of Edna Pontellier." *Southern Literary Journal* 10, no. 2 (1978): 107–22.

Kauffman, Stanley. "The Really Lost Generation." *The New Republic* 3 (December 1966): 22, 37–38.

Lattin, Patricia Hopkins. "Kate Chopin's Repeating Characters." *Mississippi Quarterly: The Journal of Southern Culture* 33 (1979–80): 19–37.

Leary, Lewis. "Kate Chopin's Other Novel." *Southern Literary Journal* 1 (Autumn 1968): 60–74.

Leder, Priscilla. "An American Dilemma: Cultural Conflict in Kate Chopin's *The Awakening.*" *Southern Studies* 22, no. 1 (1983): 97–104.

Milliner, Gladys W. "The Tragic Imperative: *The Awakening* and *The Bell Jar.*" *Mary Wollstonecraft Newsletter* 2 (December 1973): 21–27.

Rocks, James E. "Kate Chopin's Ironic Vision." *Louisiana Review* 1 (Winter 1972): 11–20.

Rosen, Kenneth M. "Kate Chopin's *The Awakening:* Ambiguity as Art." *Journal of American Studies* 5 (August 1971): 197–99.

Schuyler, William. "Kate Chopin." *Writer* 7 (August 1894): 115–17.

Seyersted, Per. "Kate Chopin: An Important St. Louis Writer Reconsidered." *The Bulletin—Missouri Historical Society* 19 (January 1963): 89–114.

Skaggs, Peggy. "Three Tragic Figures in Kate Chopin's *The Awakening.*" *Louisiana Studies* 13 (Winter 1974): 345–64.

Springer, Marlene. *Kate Chopin and Edith Wharton: An Annotated Bibliographical Guide to Secondary Materials.* Boston: G. K. Hall, 1976.

Sullivan, Ruth, and Stewart Smith. "Narrative Stance in Kate Chopin's *The Awakening.*" *Studies in American Fiction* 1 (Spring 1973): 62–75.

Toth, Emily. "Kate Chopin and Literary Convention: 'Désirée's Baby.'" *Studies in Short Fiction* 18, no. 3 (Summer 1981): 201–8.

————. "The Independent Woman and 'Free Love.'" *The Massachusetts Review* 16 (Autumn 1975): 647–64.

————. "Timely and Timeless: The Treatment of Time in *The Awakening* and *Sister Carrie.*" *Southern Studies* 16 (1977): 271–76.

Walker, Nancy. "Feminist or Naturalist: The Social Context of Kate Chopin's *The Awakening.*" *The Southern Quarterly* 17, no. 2 (1979): 95–103.

Webb, Bonnie Larson. "Four Points of Equilibrium in *The Awakening.*" *South Central Bulletin* 42, no. 4 (1982): 148–51.

Wheeler, Otis B. "The Five Awakenings of Edna Pontellier." *The Southern Review* 11 (January 1975): 118–28.

White, Robert. "Inner and Outer Space in *The Awakening.*" *Mosaic* 17, no. 1 (1984): 97–109.

Wilson, Edmund. *Patriotic Gore.* New York: Oxford University Press, 1962.

Wolff, Cynthia G. "Thanatos and Eros: Kate Chopin's *The Awakening.*" *American Quarterly* 25 (October 1973): 449–71.

Ziff, Larzer. *The American 1890s: Life and Times of a Lost Generation.* New York: Viking, 1966.

Zlotnick, Joan. "A Woman's Will: Kate Chopin on Selfhood, Wifehood, and Motherhood." *Markham Review* 3 (October 1968): 1–5.

Acknowledgments

"A Forgotten Novel" (originally entitled "A Forgotten Novel: Kate Chopin's *The Awakening*") by Kenneth Eble from *Western Humanities Review* 10, no. 3 (Summer 1956), © 1956 by the University of Utah. Reprinted by permission.

"An Abyss of Inequality" by Larzer Ziff from *The American 1890's: Life and Times of a Lost Generation* by Larzer Ziff, © 1966 by Larzer Ziff. Reprinted by permission of Viking Penguin, Inc.

"Cane River World: *At Fault* and Related Stories" (originally entitled "Cane River World: Kate Chopin's *At Fault* and Related Stories") by Donald A. Ringe from *Studies in American Fiction* 3, no. 2 (Autumn 1975), © 1975 by Northeastern University. Reprinted by permission.

"The Fiction of Limits: 'Désirée's Baby'" (originally entitled "Kate Chopin and the Fiction of Limits: 'Désirée's Baby'") by Cynthia Griffin Wolff from *Southern Literary Journal* 10, no. 2 (Spring 1978), © 1978 by the Department of English of the University of North Carolina at Chapel Hill. Reprinted by permission of the *Southern Literary Journal*.

"The Novel of Awakening" by Susan J. Rosowski from *Genre* 12, no. 3 (Fall 1979), © 1979 by the University of Oklahoma. Reprinted by permission.

"Gouvernail, Kate Chopin's Sensitive Bachelor" by Joyce C. Dyer from *Southern Literary Journal* 14, no. 1 (Fall 1981), © 1981 by the Department of English of the University of North Carolina at Chapel Hill. Reprinted by permission of the *Southern Literary Journal*.

"Kate Chopin's Sleeping Bruties" by Joyce C. Dyer from *The Markham Review* 10 (Fall/Winter 1980–81), © 1981 by Wagner College. Reprinted by permission.

"'Ripe Figs': Kate Chopin in Miniature" by Elaine Gardiner from *Modern Fiction Studies* 28, no. 3 (Autumn 1982), © 1982 by the Purdue Research Foundation. Reprinted by permission of the Purdue Research Foundation, West Lafayette, Indiana.

"The Second Coming of Aphrodite" (originally entitled "The Second Coming of Aphrodite: Kate Chopin's Fantasy of Desire") by Sandra M. Gilbert from *The*

Kenyon Review 5, no. 3 (Summer 1983), © 1983 by Kenyon College. Reprinted by permission.

"The Siren of Grand Isle: Adèle's Role in *The Awakening*" by Kathleen Margaret Lant from *Southern Studies: An Interdisciplinary Journal of the South* 23, no. 2 (Summer 1984), © 1984 by the Southern Studies Institute. Reprinted by permission.

Index

Adèle Ratignolle (*The Awakening*), 98;
as agent of Edna's despair, 104,
123; as Edna's guide, 115–19; as
extreme personality, 121; influence
of, 96, 97; as mother, 4, 22; self-
effacement of, 119–20, 121; sexuality of, 120; as symbol of femininity, 116–17

Alcée Arobin (*The Awakening*), 13–14,
22, 71, 103; shallow sexuality of,
47, 122

Anand (*Daughter of Earth*), 55

Aphrodite: Cather's view of, 110–12;
Chopin's identification with, 112–
13; Edna as image of, 101; as feminist deity, 91, 92, 108, 110; and
ocean image, 97–98; rebirth of, 3;
Sexton's view of, 112; as symbol
of erotic liberation, 109

Aphrodite (Louÿs), 104, 111

Armand ("Désirée's Baby"), 38–40

At Fault, 1; capacity for change in, 30–
33; criticism of, 17; female self-
awareness in, 20; historical background, 26–27; industrialization as
theme in, 28–29; margin as metaphor in, 41; social change as theme
in, 25; weaknesses of, 12, 19, 28,
32

Athénaise ("Athénaise"), 64–66

Austen, Jane, 58, 95

Autoeroticism, in *The Awakening,* 1–4

Awakening: to complex reality, 49, 51,
53, 57; emotional, 55, 58; through
fantasy, 102; to limitations, 43,
44–45, 55, 58, 96; metaphysical,
96; of moral sense, 57, 58;
through outward commitment, 54–
55, 56; to self-awareness, 15, 119,
120; to self-love, 2, 3–4; sexual,
14, 41, 71

Awakening, The, 1, 7–8, 11, 105; attitude toward marriage in, 23; and
Chopin's short fiction, 61; contrasts in, 84; criticism of, 7, 24,
48, 90, 91–92, 115; cyclical pattern in, 86; cynicism in, 68; dinner
party scene in, 66–67, 90–91, 92,
103–4; fantasy in, 92–93, 99–100,
102–3; female community in, 96–
97, 108; Flaubert's influence on,
20, 46, 93, 106–7; Gouvernail's
role in, 66–69; image of death in,
68; imagery in, 41–42, 66–67, 86,
94, 97; limitation theme in, 46–
48; margin as metaphor in, 41–42,
93; matriarchal mythology in, 91–
92, 98, 99, 100–101, 108; myth
of Aphrodite in, 91–92, 97; narcis-
sism in, 1–4; point of view in, 23–
24, 93–94; as "political romance,"
90; realism in, 95, 99, 103; sensuality in, 9, 12, 14, 15; strengths
and weaknesses of, 2; structure of,
12; style of, 9–10, 12–13, 92;

133

Will Ladislaw (*Middlemarch*), 58

Wolff, Cynthia Griffin, 90, 92

Women: autonomy of, 111; community of, 96–97, 108; dependence of, 45; limited roles of, 43, 48, 56–57, 59; and marriage, 23; moon as symbol of, 72–73, 74, 98; ocean as symbol of, 97–98, 107–8, 123; as possessions, 93; power of imagination of, 107; self-awareness of, 20; sexuality of, 14, 15, 71, 73, 74, 111; as victims of romantic myth, 48–50; and work, 55, 56, 120. *See also individual characters*

Woodhull, Victoria, 108

Woolf, Virginia, 93, 109, 112

Words for Dr. Y. (Sexton), 112

Wuthering Heights (E. Brontë), 95

Yeats, W. B., 112–13

Ziff, Larzer, 36